make it ahead

make it ahead

a barefoot contessa cookbook

ina garten

Photographs by Quentin Bacon

Garden photographs by John M. Hall

CLARKSON POTTER/PUBLISHERS

New York

Copyright © 2014 by Ina Garten

All rights reserved.
Published in the United States by Clarkson Potter/Publishers, an imprint of
the Crown Publishing Group, a division of Random House LLC, a Penguin
Random House Company, New York.
www.crownpublishing.com
www.clarksonpotter.com

CLARKSON POTTER is a trademark and POTTER with colophon is a
registered trademark of Random House LLC.

Library of Congress Cataloging-in-Publication Data
    Make it ahead / Ina Garten.
        pages cm — (A Barefoot Contessa cookbook)
    1. Make-ahead cooking. 2. Barefoot Contessa (Store) I. Title.
    TX714.G3644   2014
    641.5'55—dc23   2014004486

ISBN 978-0-307-46488-0
Ebook ISBN 978-0-7704-3449-6

Printed in Hong Kong

Design by Marysarah Quinn
Photographs by Quentin Bacon
Garden photographs copyright © 2014 by John M. Hall
Front jacket and title page photographs copyright © 2014 by Brigitte Lacombe
Photograph on page 236 copyright © by Joshua Greene

10 9 8 7 6 5 4 3 2 1

First Edition

contents

thank you!

When I wake up in the morning, I sometimes ask myself, "What do I feel like doing today?" Happily, the answer is, "I feel like testing recipes!" My team, Barbara Libath and Lidey Heuck, and I work really hard but we also have a wonderful time together. There is no way these recipes would be so accurate if, after I was done working on them, they didn't retest them over and over again. I'm as grateful for their constant support and counsel as I am for the joy they bring to work.

Next is the team of people at Clarkson Potter/Publishers, which has been my home since my first book; I can't imagine a happier place. I'm so grateful to Maya Mavjee, the lovely president of the Crown Group; Pam Krauss, the amazing publisher of Clarkson Potter; Marysarah Quinn, the creative director of Crown who also designs my books with such creativity; Rica Allannic, my wonderful editor; and Kate Tyler, who handles all the publicity so brilliantly. They are all extraordinary women and so good at what they do. Thank you!

Then there is the amazing team of people who help create the photographs for my books. We spend weeks on end together cooking, baking, styling, and photographing the food. Quentin Bacon takes the most gorgeous food photographs! It may look easy when he does it but anyone who has taken a snap of their dinner for Instagram knows how hard it is to make food look that luscious! Cyd McDowell and Vivian Lui cook and bake gorgeous food for the photographs—and no tricks with motor oil are allowed! (In fact, after Quentin takes the picture, we often sit down and eat it!) Thank you also to my dear friend Sarah Chase, who constantly inspires me with new ideas and recipes. And my thanks to Barb Fritz, for finding the simplest, most stylish plate or bowl for us to use. These are some of the happiest days I have working on my books. Also, John Hall is a genius at photographing my garden at all times of the year. And one of the most exciting experiences of my life was being photographed by the incomparable Brigitte Lacombe for the book cover! I will always cherish that day that we spent together.

Finally, there is the extraordinary support from my wonderful agent, Esther Newberg, who takes such good care of me so I can concentrate on writing books. And of course to my husband, Jeffrey: I can honestly say that none of this would be possible without you. Thank you for your unconditional love and your inspiration over the past fifty years.

make it ahead

When I started thinking about this book, I asked my assistant Barbara Libath, "What's the most common cooking problem that people write to us about?" "That's easy!" she exclaimed. "We get the same question all the time: 'Can I make it ahead?'" Wonderful, I thought, because I've had so much experience with cooking ahead! When I had a specialty food store in East Hampton, New York, that's basically what we did—we prepared all kinds of savory dishes and baked goods and people took them home and served them that night or the next day. During the twenty years that I ran the store, I learned so many tricks for preparing the kinds of recipes that you really *can* make ahead, and we made them in a way that ensured the food would taste fresh and delicious whenever it was served.

We all have the same dilemma—we want to entertain with ease. One of my great pleasures is cooking a wonderful meal for Jeffrey and my friends; but, like everyone else, I have so much going on that it's hard to find a whole day to cook just for the fun of it. There are two things I like about cooking ahead. First, the task of making a three-course dinner over several days seems so much less daunting and anxious-making than cooking everything on the actual day of the party. Second, when surprises happen—and they always do!—I have time to fix them. Maybe one of those onions I got for the stew is brown inside and I need to run to the store for a fresh one. Or the store was out of my favorite Pernigotti cocoa powder so I need a day or two to order it online. We've all had FedEx deliveries that got held up in a snowstorm in Memphis and arrived a day late. When it's your Thanksgiving turkey, though, you don't want to be stuck at the last minute without the main course! If I'm making everything in advance, I'm relaxed because I have time to fix a problem or even change the menu. Each recipe in this book is designed to make and serve right away, plus I give easy instructions so you know not only *how* to make it ahead but also *how far in advance* you can make it.

Of course, there is ahead of time and there's *way* ahead of time. I'm often asked some variation of "Can I bake my holiday cookies in August and defrost them for Christmas?" The answer, sadly, is no. Cookies will be soggy and tasteless after months in the freezer. What you *can* do, however, is make the dough, cut out the cookies, freeze them unbaked, and *then* bake them at Christmastime as I do with my Ginger Shortbread (page 230). Everyone who has roasted a chicken knows that if you cook it on Wednesday, refrigerate it, and serve it on Friday, it'll never taste as moist and delicious as it would have if you'd served it hot right out of the oven. On the other hand, the chicken will be *even better* if you season and prep it on Wednesday so it's ready to simply throw into the oven an hour

and a half before dinner on Friday. What's important about learning to cook ahead is to know what you can make in advance and what you need to do at the last minute. Some dishes, such as soups and stews, can be cooked ahead completely and simply reheated before dinner, but it doesn't work for everything. In this book, I'll recommend which method works best for each recipe. In addition, I've tried to include in each chapter a recipe for something that you *think* you can't make ahead, such as mashed potatoes and whipped cream, but even there, I've figured out a way!

cooking ahead

I didn't just want to write recipes that were *okay* when they're made ahead, I wanted to write recipes that were actually *better* if they're made ahead. A dish like Moroccan Lamb Tagine (page 111) derives its rich depth of flavor from roasting for hours and hours—and if you plan it right, it will be ready to serve just as your guests are sitting down to dinner. But I also include instructions on making it in advance and simply reheating it before dinner. Other recipes, like Jalapeño Margaritas (page 26) and Dark Chocolate Terrine with Orange Sauce (page 209), actually taste better after the flavors have time to meld.

I've been making dishes in advance for years—I just never thought about them as "make-ahead" dishes. When I owned my store, Barefoot Contessa, we prepared soups, salads, dinners, and desserts for our customers to take home. It didn't matter what those dishes tasted like right out of *our* oven because most people wouldn't be eating them right away. What *really* mattered to me was how those dishes were going to taste several hours—or even days—later when customers reheated them in *their* ovens to serve at home.

At the store, customers loved appetizers like Truffled Chicken Liver Mousse (page 32) that could be stored in the fridge for a week. Cauliflower & Celery Root Soup (page 54) could be quickly reheated for a satisfying lunch or dinner. Pot pies were a staple at the store. We prepared and froze them unbaked so customers could put them in the oven whenever dinner guests showed up. I've included lots of those recipes in this book, including my French Chicken Pot Pie (page 98), which is similar to my classic Barefoot Contessa chicken pot pie but has been ramped up with leeks and fresh tarragon. Another favorite at the store was Baked Polenta with Mushrooms & Blue Cheese (page 174), which we assembled and packed in baking trays so it was ready to heat and serve at home. Because we had already simmered the polenta and roasted the mushrooms, customers were able to pop the dishes into their own ovens for an easy, freshly baked dinner. The wonderful aromas wafting through the house probably weren't so bad, either! That's exactly what I want you to be able to do with the recipes in this book—to prepare them in advance and pop the dishes in the oven before dinner. Every recipe has all the tips that I learned over those years at the store.

baking ahead

Baked goods are particularly easy to make in advance, as long as you know a few tricks. Cakes such as pound cakes that are moist and dense refrigerate very well (though you want to serve them at room temperature). While cakes that are light, such as sponge cakes, freeze well, it's best to defrost them slowly overnight in the fridge. Sour Cream Corn Bread (page 239) can be baked, then sliced and toasted the next day. Even better!

Here's another reason that I love baking in advance: I'm a really messy baker! After I'm done whipping up a few cakes, I usually end up with sugar on the floor and flour all over me. When I have guests coming in five minutes, I don't want to be cleaning the kitchen or getting some stray molasses out of my hair. And, contrary to people's expectations, if you know which kinds of recipes to choose, baking ahead doesn't have to result in gooey messes and weeping frosting.

My Lemon Poppy Seed Cake (page 219) is delicious when it comes out of the oven but the recipe includes a lemon syrup that soaks into the cake while it is cooling and a lemon glaze that brightens its flavors even more. Best of all, if it's stored properly, the cake is actually *moister* and more lemony the next day. And then there's breakfast! Who wants to get up at 5am to surprise houseguests with something special for breakfast? At Barefoot Contessa, where we baked thousands of muffins every day, I discovered that if we mixed the muffin batters the

night before and scooped them into muffin pans the next day, we could have freshly baked muffins all day long. The best part is that the muffins tasted exactly the same as if we'd whipped up a new batch of batter each time we baked them. The same system works at home. Blueberry Bran Muffins (page 256) can be mixed the night before and baked the next morning so you can serve hot muffins when you're still half asleep. All the pleasures of freshly baked muffins and no mess!

entertaining ahead

Recently, I had a dinner party for eight and I made a plan to cook everything ahead. My goals were that each recipe be prepared almost completely and that the only instructions I would need in the last hour could fit on a yellow Post-it note. First, I made Warm Fig & Arugula Salad (page 50). I prepped the greens and whisked the vinaigrette and refrigerated them separately. Just before dinner, I roasted the walnuts and figs for a few minutes, tossed the greens and vinaigrette, and put the warm fruit and nuts on top.

Next, for the main course, I made Slow-Roasted Spiced Pork (page 106), Maple Baked Beans (from *Barefoot Contessa at Home*), and Winter Slaw (page 77). The pork and baked beans each roasted for 6 or 7 hours, and I prepped all the components of the slaw in advance: The kale, radicchio, Brussels sprouts, and shaved Parmesan went into plastic bags and the lemon vinaigrette went into a container and they all went into the fridge. When the pork was done, I sliced it onto a big serving platter with wedges of lime, the baked beans were served in the Le Creuset pot they cooked in, and the slaw ingredients were simply tossed together in a big bowl. Easy!

Finally, for dessert, I made Coffee Granita (page 191), which was light and refreshing after the rich pork dinner. All I needed to do was take the granita out of the freezer, scrape it with a fork, and serve it in martini glasses with a big dollop of whipped cream—which, of course, I'd also made ahead. An hour before dinner—when I'm usually saying to Jeffrey, *"Don't talk to me!"*—I literally had nothing to do. I almost felt guilty, but it was wonderful. You can imagine how pleased I was when one of my guests not only commented that it was one of the best dinners he'd ever eaten, but also asked if I would make the same menu again next Saturday!

I was hooked. I could actually give a dinner party and not be completely exhausted by the time the first guest arrived. The meal was not only *okay*, in fact, it was *even better* because I'd made it ahead! Who wouldn't want all their dinner parties to be like that?

prepping ahead

One of the key things I've explored in this book is how to prep ingredients ahead of time—from cutting and storing butternut squash to assembling the dry ingredients for a cake. It seems as though each ingredient has its own process. Basil leaves can be prepped three days ahead by washing them, drying them very well, and refrigerating them with a slightly damp paper towel in a plastic bag, but I save the final chopping for the last minute or the leaves will turn brown. Cut potatoes won't turn brown for days in the fridge if they're stored in a big bowl of water. Asparagus is best stored upright with the cut ends in water (like flowers) or wrapped with a damp towel and placed in a plastic storage bag. When I'm baking, for some recipes like the Fresh Apple Spice Cake (page 195), I find that I can combine the wet ingredients in the recipe and refrigerate them and combine the dry ingredients and store them at room temperature. Before dinner, I simply mix the two together, add the apples, raisins, and pecans, and bake the cake. Almost all of the work is done in advance, but I can still have a delicious warm cake right out of the oven to serve my guests for dessert.

using this book

Each recipe in this book has instructions for making the dish as if you were going to serve it immediately and then a note explaining how to make it ahead, if that's what you want to do. Many recipes have processes for making them ahead built right in, such as my Overnight Belgian Waffles (page 248), where the batter sits overnight at room temperature to allow the yeasty flavor to develop. The Marinated Herbed Feta (page 36) needs a few days in the fridge so the spices and herbs really permeate the cheese. If you thought you couldn't make a roast chicken ahead, you'll love my Roast Chicken with Bread & Arugula Salad (page 95). You season the chicken two days in advance so the flavors get into the meat before you roast it, and then you bake it right on top of bread slices, which then become croutons on the salad. For my Easy Coquilles Saint Jacques (page 133) the only last-minute instruction you'll need is "Bake for 20 minutes at 400 degrees." For the Bruschettas with Sautéed Chard (page 61), you'll simply need to toast the bread and reheat the chard. Writing this book has taught me how to think about making dishes ahead of time in a whole new way. I hope you'll find not only that the recipes are foolproof and delicious, but also that entertaining is less stressful and more fun. After all, isn't that what dinner parties are supposed to be all about?!

xxx's Ina

Whole Wheat Peanut Butter Dog Biscuits
MAKES 10 TO 20 BISCUITS

Everyone in the house needs homemade treats, even your best friend! We tested these dog "bones" against the ones from the grocery store and they won every time! All of our test subjects made a beeline for these. Hope your dog will, too!

1½ cups stone-ground whole wheat flour
1 cup all-purpose flour
½ cup powdered milk
½ cup quick-cooking oats (not instant), plus extra for sprinkling
½ cup smooth peanut butter
2 tablespoons toasted wheat germ
1 extra-large egg, lightly beaten
1 egg beaten with 1 tablespoon water, for egg wash

Preheat the oven to 325 degrees. Line a sheet pan with parchment paper.

In the bowl of an electric mixer fitted with the paddle attachment, combine the two flours, the powdered milk, oats, peanut butter, and wheat germ. With the mixer on low speed, add the egg and 1 cup of water and mix just until it forms a slightly sticky ball.

Dump the dough out on a well-floured board (I use all-purpose flour) and knead it into a ball. Roll the dough out ½ inch thick. Dip a dog bone–shaped cookie cutter in flour and cut out shapes. Collect the scraps, knead lightly, roll out again, and cut more dog biscuits.

Place the biscuits on the prepared sheet pan and brush with the egg wash. Sprinkle with oats and bake for 1 hour, until completely hard. Cool and toss!

MAKE IT AHEAD: Prepare completely and store at room temperature in an airtight container for up to a week.

cocktails

Summer Rosé Sangria

Jalapeño Margaritas

Cranberry Martinis

Parmesan Kale Chips

Roasted Red Pepper Hummus

Truffled Chicken Liver Mousse

Greek Mezze Platter with
Thyme Roasted Red Peppers

Marinated Herbed Feta

new year's eve in paris

Every year, Jeffrey and I spend New Year's Eve in Paris with friends. We hire a taxi to drive us all over the city at night to see the sights lit up for the holidays. We take a bottle of Champagne to drink on the steps of Sacré Coeur with the Eiffel Tower sparkling like a diamond in the background. We walk across the Seine on the Pont des Arts and marvel at the view of the Louvre museum all illuminated. And finally, we stop at the Hemingway Bar at the Ritz for a delicious cocktail to warm us up. Then at around 11pm, we all come home for an elegant late-night supper. It sounds wonderful and romantic, doesn't it?

But oops! There's a problem! Of course, I want to cook a memorable dinner on New Year's Eve but how can I do that when I've been out carousing with Jeffrey and our friends all night?! This is what I do—I make the dinner ahead! Before we leave the house, I prepare all the ingredients I need for an elegant pasta or stew that will be easy to finish cooking the minute I get home. One year I made Lemon Capellini with Caviar from *The Barefoot Contessa Cookbook*. I prepped the lemon and butter sauce in advance and simply left it in the pan near the stove. When we arrived home, I boiled a large pot of water and reheated the sauce. A package of DeCecco capellini literally takes only 3 minutes to cook! I drained the pasta, then cooked it in the sauce for two minutes, plated it, and added a big dollop of caviar on each serving. It was so delicious and very "New Year's Eve in Paris."

This year, I'm going to make my Provençal Fish Stew (page 137). I'll cook the soup stock and make the garlicky rouille and toasts in advance. When we get home before midnight, all I'll need to do is reheat the soup, add the fish and mussels, and cook the stew for 10 minutes. We'll all have big steaming bowls of seafood with a dollop of rouille and some crusty bread for a very Parisian dinner. (I secretly love that no one can figure out how I get dinner on the table in 15 minutes without having a total meltdown.) Elegant New Year's Eve dinner and no stress. Now that's something to celebrate!

Summer Rosé Sangria serves 6

Everyone who lived through the 1970s has had Spanish sangria with red wine, orange, and spices. I've updated that old cliché with a combination of rosé wine, fresh berries, and plums. A splash of Grand Marnier liqueur and some Cognac add just the right balance of sweet and fruity.

1 (750 ml) bottle good rosé wine
½ cup Pom Wonderful pomegranate juice
⅓ cup freshly squeezed lemon juice (3 lemons)
¼ cup superfine sugar
3 tablespoons Grand Marnier
1 tablespoon Cognac or brandy
Water and ice, plus extra ice for serving
½ cup fresh raspberries
8 large fresh strawberries, hulled and quartered
2 red plums, pitted and sliced ¼ inch thick

If you can find it, I love Robert Sinskey Vin Gris; but, of course, you can use any good rosé wine.

Combine the rosé, pomegranate juice, lemon juice, sugar, Grand Marnier, Cognac, 1 cup of water, and 1 cup of ice in a large glass pitcher. Stir in the raspberries, strawberries, and plums, cover, and refrigerate for at least 2 hours but preferably overnight.

When ready to serve, fill wine goblets or highball glasses halfway with ice. Pour the sangria over the ice, spooning some of the macerated fruit into each glass. Serve ice cold.

MAKE IT AHEAD: Prepare the sangria and refrigerate for up to 24 hours. Pour over ice and serve cold.

Jalapeño Margaritas MAKES 6 DRINKS

My editor and friend Pam Krauss took me to the John Dory Oyster Bar in New York City and we ordered delicious jalapeño margaritas. I love the contrast of the ice-cold drink with the heat of the jalapeños. These are mildly hot but, of course, you can use more peppers and make them even hotter! Infuse the tequila with the jalapeño overnight; any longer and it will become too spicy.

1 small jalapeño pepper (or half a large jalapeño)
1½ cups silver tequila, such as Avión
1 cup Triple Sec
1 cup freshly squeezed lime juice (8 limes)
¼ cup freshly squeezed lemon juice (2 lemons)
2 tablespoons honey
Pinch of kosher salt
Ice

Pierce the jalapeño pepper in 8 to 10 places with the tip of a sharp paring knife and cut it in half lengthwise, leaving the seeds and the ribs. Place the pepper in a 4-cup liquid measuring cup, pour in the tequila, cover with plastic wrap, and allow to sit at room temperature for 24 hours.

Discard the jalapeño and pour the tequila into a pitcher through a sieve to remove the seeds. Add the Triple Sec, lime juice, lemon juice, honey, and salt and stir. Use immediately or cover and refrigerate for up to 6 hours.

When ready to serve, fill 6 margarita glasses with ice and pour over the margarita mixture; or fill a cocktail shaker with ice and some of the mixture, shake vigorously for 30 seconds, and pour into glasses. Serve ice cold.

MAKE IT AHEAD: Prepare the entire cocktail mixture and refrigerate for up to 6 hours. Pour over ice or shake with ice before serving.

Cranberry Martinis makes 6 drinks

Last November, I filmed a Food Network special called Thanksgiving Live *to answer viewers' questions about cooking Thanksgiving dinner. Bobby Flay made a delicious cranberry martini to sip while we worked (what a good idea!). They look so festive and my guests loved them! Infuse the vodka with the orange zest and cranberries at least 2 days ahead.*

1 cup sugar

1 cup fresh cranberries

6 (1 × 3-inch) strips of orange zest, plus extra for serving (see note)

1 (750 ml) bottle good vodka, such as Grey Goose

1 cup cranberry juice cocktail, preferably tart

¼ cup Triple Sec

Ice

Several days ahead, place the sugar, cranberries, 6 strips of orange zest, and 1 cup of water in a small saucepan. Bring to a boil, lower the heat, and simmer for 5 minutes, until the cranberries start to pop open. Pour the vodka into a large pitcher, add the cranberry mixture, and store covered in the refrigerator for at least 2 days and up to 5 days.

When ready to serve, strain the vodka mixture, reserving the cranberries and discarding the orange zest. Stir in the cranberry juice cocktail and Triple Sec. Fill a cocktail shaker with ice, add the drink mixture, shake for a full 30 seconds (it's longer than you think!), and strain into martini glasses. Rub the rim of each glass with fresh orange zest, spoon a few cranberries into each glass, and serve ice cold.

I use a vegetable peeler to make strips of orange zest.

MAKE IT AHEAD: Prepare the entire cocktail mixture and refrigerate for up to 3 days. Shake with ice before serving.

Parmesan Kale Chips SERVES 6

Kale is a delicious vegetable that seems to be everywhere now. If you can find flat kale—sometimes labeled cavalo nero, Dinosaur kale, or lacinato—it can be roasted for the perfect light bite to serve with drinks. It's simply kale, olive oil, and salt, and it roasts in 15 minutes. Of course, freshly grated Parmesan cheese makes everything taste better.

1 large bunch flat-leaf kale
Good olive oil
Kosher salt
Freshly grated Parmesan cheese

Preheat the oven to 350 degrees. Line 2 sheet pans with parchment paper.

With a sharp knife, remove and discard the hard rib from the center of each leaf, leaving the leaves as intact as possible. Place them on the sheet pans, drizzle or brush them with olive oil, and toss to coat lightly. Sprinkle generously with salt and bake for 10 minutes, until crispy. Sprinkle lightly with Parmesan cheese and bake for another 5 minutes. Cool and serve.

MAKE IT AHEAD: Prepare and cool to room temperature. Wrap tightly and store at room temperature for up to 4 days.

Roasted Red Pepper Hummus

At Barefoot Contessa, we made gallons of hummus every day. I think it's even more irresistible made with roasted red peppers and a touch of Sriracha for heat.

1 (29-ounce) can chickpeas, drained (3 cups)
½ cup freshly squeezed lemon juice (3 lemons)
⅓ cup sesame tahini
2 tablespoons chopped garlic (6 cloves)
1½ teaspoons Sriracha
2 roasted red bell peppers (page 35)
Kosher salt and freshly ground black pepper
Good olive oil
2 tablespoons toasted pine nuts (see note), for serving
Toasted pita triangles (see note) and fresh vegetables,
    for serving

To toast the pita triangles, arrange on sheet pans, brush with olive oil, sprinkle with salt and pepper, and bake at 375 degrees for 8 to 10 minutes.

Toast pine nuts in a dry sauté pan over low heat, tossing often, for 5 to 10 minutes.

Place the chickpeas, lemon juice, tahini, garlic, Sriracha, roasted red peppers, 1 tablespoon salt, and 1 teaspoon pepper in the bowl of a food processor fitted with the steel blade. Process until the mixture is coarsely puréed. Taste for seasonings, and transfer to a serving bowl. Drizzle with olive oil, sprinkle with toasted pine nuts, and serve cold or at room temperature with pita triangles and vegetables.

MAKE IT AHEAD: Prepare the hummus, cover, and refrigerate for up to a week.

Truffled Chicken Liver Mousse

MAKES 1 LARGE OR 4 SMALL RAMEKINS

Chicken liver pâté was one of the first things I remember making for a dinner party after Jeffrey and I were married. It's easy to prepare and it keeps in the fridge for at least a week. This updated version of that original pâté, flavored with fresh thyme, truffle butter, and Cognac, is so good!

1¼ pounds fresh chicken livers, fat and membranes trimmed
1 cup whole milk
8 tablespoons (1 stick) unsalted butter, at room temperature, divided
1½ cups chopped yellow onion (1 large)
1 teaspoon fresh thyme leaves
¼ cup Cognac or brandy
Kosher salt and freshly ground black pepper
3 ounces white truffle butter, at room temperature (see note)
½ cup minced fresh flat-leaf parsley, plus extra sprigs
3 to 4 tablespoons melted duck fat or clarified butter (see note)
Crackers or toast triangles, for serving

I buy containers of white truffle butter and duck fat from DArtagnan.com.

To clarify butter, heat the butter until melted and pour into a glass measuring cup. When the solids settle to the bottom, pour off the clear golden liquid, which is clarified butter, and discard the solids.

Place the chicken livers and milk in a medium bowl, cover, and refrigerate for at least 2 hours. Drain the livers and discard the milk.

Melt 4 tablespoons of the butter in a medium (10-inch) skillet over medium heat. Add the onion and cook for 8 to 10 minutes, stirring occasionally, until tender but not browned. Add the chicken livers and thyme and cook for 4 to 5 minutes, turning with tongs to cook evenly, until they're lightly browned on the outside but still raw inside. Add the Cognac, 1 tablespoon salt, and 2 teaspoons pepper and continue to cook for 3 to 4 minutes, until the livers are cooked but still very pink inside. (If they're overcooked, the pâté will be dry.) Pour the contents of the pan into the bowl of a food processor fitted with the steel blade and allow to cool for 15 minutes.

Pulse the processor until the chicken livers are almost smooth. Dice the remaining 4 tablespoons of butter and add to the bowl.

MAKE IT AHEAD: Prepare the pâté, wrap, and refrigerate for up to a week.

Add the truffle butter and process until smooth. Add the parsley and pulse just to incorporate.

Pour the mousse into one large or four small (8-ounce) ramekins. Pour a thin layer of melted duck fat or clarified butter on each mousse and place whole parsley sprigs on top. Refrigerate for at least 6 hours. Allow to sit at room temperature for 15 minutes before serving with crackers or warm toasts.

Greek Mezze Platter with Thyme Roasted Red Peppers SERVES 8 TO 10

A Greek mezze platter is a dramatic dish to put out with drinks. I serve it with small plates and forks and let everyone help themselves.

6 large Holland red bell peppers
3 tablespoons good olive oil
3 tablespoons freshly squeezed lemon juice
6 sprigs fresh thyme
Sea salt or fleur de sel
Roasted Red Pepper Hummus (page 30) or store-bought hummus
Marinated Herbed Feta (page 36)
Easy Tzatziki (page 122)
Kalamata olives
Stuffed grape leaves, store-bought
Toasted pita triangles (page 30), for serving

Preheat the oven to 500 degrees. Line a sheet pan with aluminum foil.

Place the peppers on the sheet pan and roast for 30 to 35 minutes, until the skins are completely wrinkled and the peppers are very charred, turning them twice during roasting. Remove the pan from the oven and immediately wrap the entire pan tightly with aluminum foil. Set aside for 30 minutes, until the peppers are cool enough to handle. Remove the stems and cut in quarters lengthwise. Remove and discard the skin and seeds.

Place the peppers in a shallow dish and add the olive oil, lemon juice, thyme sprigs, and ¾ teaspoon salt. Wrap the dish and refrigerate for at least 24 hours. Sprinkle the peppers with sea salt and arrange them artfully on a platter with the hummus, feta, tzatziki, olives, grape leaves, and pita.

MAKE IT AHEAD: Prepare the peppers completely and refrigerate for up to a week. Assemble the platter up to 4 hours ahead, wrap, and store at room temperature.

Marinated Herbed Feta SERVES 8

Most marinated feta consists of cubes of feta swimming in a large jar of olive oil, which I think makes the feta oily. Instead, I slice it and sprinkle it with thyme, fennel, crushed red pepper, and a drizzle of olive oil. The flavor is much cleaner and brighter. Serve this with toasted pita triangles or on a Greek mezze platter with hummus (page 30), olives, and stuffed grape leaves.

I use Olio Santo olive oil.

1½ teaspoons dried thyme
½ teaspoon dried fennel seeds
½ teaspoon crushed red pepper flakes
1½ pounds Greek feta, drained and sliced ½ inch thick
3 sprigs fresh thyme
½ cup green olives with pits, such as Cerignola
½ cup good olive oil
Kosher salt and freshly ground black pepper
Toasted pita triangles (page 30), for serving

Combine the dried thyme, fennel seeds, and red pepper flakes in a small bowl. Lay the feta slices overlapping on a 9 × 9-inch square serving plate.

Sprinkle the feta with the entire herb mixture. Nestle the thyme sprigs and olives among the feta slices. Drizzle with the olive oil and sprinkle with ½ teaspoon salt and ¼ teaspoon black pepper. Cover the dish with plastic wrap and refrigerate for at least 4 hours. Serve at room temperature with the pita triangles.

MAKE IT AHEAD: Prepare the feta, wrap, and refrigerate for up to a week.

Caesar Salad with
Blue Cheese & Bacon

Zucchini Basil Soup

Spanish Tapas Peppers

Warm Fig & Arugula Salad

Wild Mushroom & Farro Soup

Cauliflower & Celery Root Soup

Tomatoes & Burrata

Bruschettas with Sautéed Chard

10 make-ahead tips for parties

1. A week ahead, instead of keeping everything in your head, write down a game plan for both the week and the day of the party.

2. A week ahead, shop for the pantry ingredients. Shop for the fresh ingredients the day before the party.

3. A week ahead, order cookies with people's names on them for place cards. I order decorated cookies from EliZabar.com.

4. Three days ahead, set the table, as long as it's not a table you ordinarily use during the week.

5. Up to a few days ahead, prep as many ingredients as possible and store them in plastic bags in the fridge.

6. Two days ahead, arrange the flowers so the petals have time to fully open up.

7. A day ahead, uncork, taste, and chill (if appropriate) the wines.

8. A day ahead, pull the platters and serving pieces you'll need and place Post-it notes on each one to remind yourself which food goes where.

9. A few hours ahead, put ground coffee and water in the coffee-maker (but don't turn it on until you're ready to serve dessert).

10. Before the party, run the dishwasher and empty it so you're ready for the cleanup afterward.

Caesar Salad with
Blue Cheese & Bacon SERVES 6

Of course, there are a million recipes for Caesar salad, but this composed
version looks gorgeous. You can make all the components ahead, then soft-
boil the eggs and assemble the salad. The runny egg and garlicky dressing
are delicious with the smoky, crisp bacon and creamy blue cheese.

6 thick-cut slices applewood-smoked bacon
6 extra-large eggs
12 (½-inch-thick) diagonally cut slices of baguette
Good olive oil
1 large garlic clove, cut in half
1 pound hearts of romaine lettuce, washed and spun dry
8 ounces good Roquefort cheese, sliced
Caesar Salad Dressing (recipe follows)
Kosher salt and freshly ground black pepper

Preheat the oven to 375 degrees.

Arrange the bacon in a single layer on a baking rack set on a
sheet pan and bake for 25 to 30 minutes, until browned. Transfer
to a plate lined with paper towels.

Meanwhile, place the eggs in a medium saucepan, fill with
water to cover by one inch, and bring to a rolling boil. Lower the
heat and simmer for exactly 4 minutes. Drain and place the eggs
in cold water for 10 minutes. Peel.

Arrange the bread slices on a sheet pan and brush the tops
with olive oil. Toast in the oven along with the bacon for 8 to
10 minutes, until golden brown. Cool for one minute, then rub
each toast with the cut side of the garlic clove. Set aside.

Cut the eggs in half lengthwise. Arrange the lettuce, bacon,
soft-boiled eggs, and Roquefort artfully on 6 salad plates. Drizzle
with the dressing and add the toasts. Sprinkle with salt and pepper and serve at room temperature.

MAKE IT AHEAD: Prepare the
lettuce and dressing and refrigerate separately for up to 3 days.
Roast the bacon, cook the eggs,
toast the bread, and assemble
before serving.

Caesar Salad Dressing MAKES 2½ CUPS

This is my classic Caesar salad dressing. It lasts for days in the refrigerator.

   1 extra-large egg yolk, at room temperature
   2 teaspoons Dijon mustard
   2 teaspoons chopped garlic (2 cloves)
   8 to 10 anchovy fillets (optional)
   ½ cup freshly squeezed lemon juice (3 lemons)
   Kosher salt and freshly ground black pepper
   1½ cups good olive oil
   ½ cup freshly grated Parmesan cheese

Place the egg yolk, mustard, garlic, anchovies (if using), lemon juice, 2 teaspoons salt, and ½ teaspoon pepper in the bowl of a food processor fitted with the steel blade. Process until smooth. With the food processor running, slowly pour the olive oil through the feed tube and process until thick. Add the Parmesan and pulse 3 times to combine.

Zucchini Basil Soup SERVES 6

Why is it that one day the zucchinis in my garden are one inch long and when I come back the next morning, they're the size of baseball bats? When they're too large to simply sauté as a side dish for dinner, I make this delicious soup that's flavored with onions, garlic, and fresh basil, and enriched with Greek yogurt.

¼ cup good olive oil, plus extra for serving
1½ cups chopped yellow onion (1 large onion)
2 tablespoons minced garlic (6 cloves)
3 pounds zucchini (unpeeled), ¾-inch-diced
½ teaspoon ground nutmeg
⅛ teaspoon crushed red pepper flakes
Kosher salt and freshly ground black pepper
1 cup good dry white wine, such as Pinot Grigio
4 cups good chicken stock, preferably homemade (page 62)
1 cup chopped fresh basil leaves, lightly packed
½ cup freshly grated Parmesan cheese
½ cup Greek yogurt, plus extra for serving
Shaved Parmesan, for serving

Using a food mill will give this soup more texture than using a blender.

Heat the olive oil in a large pot or Dutch oven over medium heat. Add the onion and sauté over medium-low heat for 8 to 10 minutes, until translucent but not browned. Add the garlic and cook for one minute. Add the zucchini, nutmeg, red pepper flakes, 1 tablespoon salt, and 1 teaspoon black pepper and sauté for 5 to 10 minutes, until the zucchini is tender.

Add the wine, chicken stock, and basil, bring it to a boil, lower the heat, and simmer uncovered for 30 minutes, until the zucchini is very tender. Pass the soup through a food mill fitted with the coarsest blade (you can also use an immersion or regular blender but the soup will have less texture). Return to the pot and bring to a simmer. Off the heat, whisk in the grated Parmesan and yogurt. Check for seasonings and serve hot topped with a dollop of yogurt, shaved Parmesan, and a drizzle of olive oil.

MAKE IT AHEAD: Prepare the soup without the Parmesan and yogurt, and refrigerate for up to 5 days or freeze for up to 3 months. Reheat the soup, whisk in the Parmesan and yogurt, and serve.

Spanish Tapas Peppers SERVES 6 TO 8

Roasting brings out the sweetness in bell peppers. This is the kind of dish served at Spanish tapas bars—slices of red and yellow peppers are filled with garlic, green olives, golden raisins, spicy saffron, and bread crumbs. A nice glass of Spanish sherry would be delicious with it.

½ cup cream sherry

½ cup golden raisins

3 Holland red bell peppers

2 Holland yellow bell peppers

Kosher salt and freshly ground black pepper

1 tablespoon minced garlic (3 cloves)

¾ cup chopped green pitted olives (4 to 6 ounces with pits)

8 oil-packed anchovy fillets, drained and minced

1 large tomato, seeded and diced

1 scant teaspoon saffron threads, crumbled

⅔ cup coarse fresh bread crumbs from a baguette
  (crusts removed)

⅓ cup good olive oil

Minced fresh flat-leaf parsley

Preheat the oven to 375 degrees.

Combine the sherry and raisins in a small saucepan, bring to a boil, and simmer for 5 minutes, until most of the liquid has evaporated. Set aside.

Meanwhile, cut each pepper in half through the core and remove the ribs and seeds. Cut each half lengthwise into 3 wedges and arrange them cut side up in a single layer in two large shallow oven-to-table baking dishes. Sprinkle with 1 teaspoon salt.

In a medium bowl, combine the steeped raisins, garlic, olives, anchovies, tomato, saffron, bread crumbs, olive oil, 1 teaspoon salt, and 1 teaspoon pepper. Spread about a tablespoon of the mixture on each pepper wedge. Bake for 35 to 40 minutes, until the peppers are tender and the filling is a little crisp on top. Sprinkle with parsley and serve warm or at room temperature.

MAKE IT AHEAD: Prepare the peppers with the filling, cover, and refrigerate for up to 24 hours. Bake before serving.

Warm Fig & Arugula Salad SERVES 6

When figs are ripe, at the end of the summer, I can't get enough of them! Unfortunately, the ones I find at the grocery store are often under-ripe; but a few minutes in the oven brings out their sweetness. I adore the combination of warm roasted figs, cold peppery arugula, piquant blue cheese, and crunchy toasted walnuts.

¼ cup aged sherry vinegar
1½ teaspoons Dijon mustard
½ teaspoon honey
Kosher salt and freshly ground black pepper
½ cup good olive oil
8 to 12 ripe fresh figs, depending on their size (see note)
1 cup whole walnut halves (4 ounces)
8 to 10 cups baby arugula (9 ounces)
8 ounces crumbled Roquefort cheese

Figs sold singly in trays will be larger than figs sold in pint baskets.

Preheat the oven to 375 degrees.

In a small bowl, whisk together the vinegar, mustard, honey, 1 teaspoon salt, and ½ teaspoon pepper. While whisking, slowly add the olive oil. Set aside.

Remove the stems from the figs with a small knife. Depending on their sizes, cut the figs in half or quarters through the stem end. Place the figs and walnuts together in a single layer on a sheet pan and roast for 5 to 15 minutes, depending on the ripeness of the figs, until they begin to release some of their juices.

Meanwhile, place the arugula in a large bowl, add the vinaigrette, and toss well. Distribute the arugula among 6 salad plates, add the Roquefort, and then place the warm figs and walnuts on top. Serve immediately.

MAKE IT AHEAD: Prep the arugula, make the vinaigrette, and crumble the blue cheese. Refrigerate separately for up to 3 days. Before serving, roast the figs and walnuts and assemble the salads.

Wild Mushroom & Farro Soup SERVES 6

Pearled farro is a whole grain that is now available in most grocery and health food stores. This soup with mushrooms, pancetta, and lots of vegetables is really hearty. I make it ahead, refrigerate it, and then reheat it, serving it with a dollop of crème fraîche and a swirl of Marsala wine. It's warm and comforting on a cold day.

Be sure you buy "pearled" farro; regular farro takes much longer to cook.

1½ ounces dried wild mushrooms, such as morels or porcini
3 tablespoons good olive oil
4 ounces pancetta, ½-inch-diced
3 cups chopped yellow onions (2 onions)
2 cups (½-inch-diced) carrots (3 to 4 carrots)
2 cups (½-inch-diced) celery (3 to 4 stalks)
4 teaspoons minced garlic (4 cloves)
¾ cup pearled farro (5 ounces) (see note)
12 ounces fresh cremini mushrooms, cleaned, stems
   discarded, ¼-inch-sliced
½ cup plus 2 tablespoons dry Marsala wine
4 cups canned beef broth, such as College Inn
3 large sprigs fresh thyme, tied together with kitchen twine
Kosher salt and freshly ground black pepper
2 tablespoons all-purpose flour
2 tablespoons unsalted butter, at room temperature
4 ounces crème fraîche
¼ cup minced fresh flat-leaf parsley

Place the dried mushrooms and 6 cups of water in a medium pot and bring to a boil. Turn off the heat, cover, and set aside for at least 20 minutes.

Meanwhile, heat the olive oil in a large pot or Dutch oven. Add the pancetta, onions, carrots, and celery and sauté over medium heat for 10 minutes, stirring occasionally, until the vegetables are tender. Add the garlic and farro and cook for 2 minutes, stirring occasionally. Add the cremini mushrooms and the ½ cup Marsala and cook for 5 to 7 minutes, until the mushrooms have released some of their liquid.

MAKE IT AHEAD: Prepare the soup completely. Refrigerate for up to a week or freeze for up to 3 months. Reheat before serving.

Meanwhile, strain the dried mushrooms through cheesecloth, reserving the liquid. Coarsely chop the mushrooms and add them to the pot, along with the strained soaking liquid, the beef broth, thyme, 2 teaspoons salt, and 1 teaspoon pepper. Bring to a boil, lower the heat, and simmer partially covered for 45 minutes, until the farro is tender. Discard the thyme bundle.

In a small bowl, mash together the flour and butter and stir into the hot soup. Simmer for 5 minutes, then stir in the crème fraîche and remaining 2 tablespoons of Marsala, and taste for seasonings. Sprinkle with the parsley and serve hot.

Cauliflower & Celery Root Soup serves 5 to 6

This is one of the most surprising soups. It tastes rich and velvety and yet, with only two tablespoons of cream in it, it's a healthy vegetable soup. Celery root and fennel give it a wonderful depth of flavor and the homemade croutons and drizzle of olive oil at the end are delicious additions.

Fennel adds a very subtle layer of flavor to the cauliflower and celery root.

¼ cup good olive oil, plus extra for serving
2 cups chopped yellow onions (2 onions)
2 cups (1-inch-diced) celery root
2 cups (1-inch-diced) fennel, core and stalks removed
2 pounds cauliflower, cored and cut into florets (1 medium)
2 cups good chicken stock, preferably homemade (page 62)
Kosher salt
2 tablespoons heavy cream
Homemade Croutons, for serving (recipe follows)
Chopped fresh chives, for serving

Heat the olive oil in a heavy-bottomed pot or Dutch oven, such as Le Creuset. Add the onions and sauté over medium-low heat for 8 to 10 minutes, stirring occasionally, until tender but not browned. Stir in the celery root and fennel and sauté for 5 minutes, stirring occasionally. Add the cauliflower, chicken stock, and 2 teaspoons of salt. Bring to a boil, lower the heat, cover, and simmer for 25 to 30 minutes, until the vegetables are very tender. Add 3 cups of water, bring to a boil, lower the heat, and simmer uncovered for 20 minutes.

Working in batches, purée the soup in a blender, until very smooth. (Don't fill the blender more than half full or it will overflow!) Pour the blended soup into a large saucepan, stir in the cream, and add 1 or 2 teaspoons of salt, depending on the saltiness of the chicken stock. Reheat the soup over medium-low heat. Ladle into soup bowls, sprinkle with croutons and chives, and drizzle with olive oil. Serve hot.

MAKE IT AHEAD: Prepare the soup and refrigerate for up to 1 week or freeze for up to 3 months. Reheat before serving. Make the croutons up to 5 days ahead.

Homemade Croutons MAKES ABOUT 2 CUPS

I stash leftover bread in the freezer and use it to make these croutons.

2 tablespoons good olive oil
2 cups (½-inch-diced) bread from a country loaf, crusts
    removed
Kosher salt

Heat the olive oil in a large (10-inch) sauté pan until hot. Add the bread and cook over medium heat, tossing frequently, until the bread is evenly toasted and browned. Sprinkle with salt.

Garlic Toasts MAKES 20 TO 25 TOASTS

This is a great way to use up leftover baguettes. They're wonderful to serve on top of soup, but you can also serve them with dips and cheeses.

1 baguette
¼ cup good olive oil
Kosher salt and freshly ground black pepper
1 garlic clove, halved lengthwise

Preheat the oven to 400 degrees.

Slice the baguette diagonally into ¼-inch-thick slices. Depending on the size of the baguette, you should get 20 to 25 slices.

Lay the slices in one layer on a baking sheet, brush each with olive oil, and sprinkle generously with salt and pepper. Bake the toasts for 15 to 20 minutes, until they are browned and crisp. As soon as they are cool enough to handle, rub one side of the toasts with the cut side of the garlic. Serve at room temperature.

MAKE IT AHEAD: You can prepare these a day or two in advance. Cool, then wrap well or store in plastic bags at room temperature.

Tomatoes & Burrata SERVES 4

Burrata is fresh Italian mozzarella with a creamy center. What else does it need besides sweet ripe tomatoes, spicy basil, and a drizzle of syrupy balsamic vinegar? I think a garlicky toasted crouton is the perfect accompaniment.

2 (8- to 10-ounce) balls of fresh burrata cheese
16 to 20 (2-inch diameter) heirloom tomatoes
Good olive oil
Aged balsamic vinegar
Kosher salt and freshly ground black pepper
20 fresh basil leaves, julienned
Fleur de sel or sea salt
Garlic Toasts (page 57)

Cut each ball of cheese in half crosswise and place the halves, cut side down, on 4 salad plates. Cut each tomato in half through the stem end and distribute them around the burrata. Drizzle the tomatoes and burrata generously with olive oil and balsamic vinegar and sprinkle with kosher salt and pepper. Scatter the basil on the salads, sprinkle with fleur de sel, and serve with Garlic Toasts.

To clean basil ahead, wash the leaves and dry them in a salad spinner. Place the whole leaves in a plastic bag with a slightly damp paper towel and refrigerate.

MAKE IT AHEAD: Make the toasts up to a day ahead. Assemble the salads when ready to serve.

Bruschettas with Sautéed Chard serves 4

Jeffrey and I visited Florence with our dearest friends and went to Cantinetta Antinori for lunch. I had bruschetta with sautéed greens and I came right home to try it with fresh chard from my garden. I love the crisp garlicky bread piled high with the warm sautéed greens, plus a squeeze of fresh lemon juice and a drizzle of fruity olive oil.

Kosher salt and freshly ground black pepper
3 pounds fresh green or rainbow chard (4 bunches)
Good olive oil
2 large garlic cloves, thinly sliced
1 round country bread, halved and sliced crosswise
    ½-inch thick
1 garlic clove, cut in half
1 lemon
Freshly grated Parmesan cheese
Fleur de sel, for serving

Bring a very large pot of water to a boil and add 1 tablespoon of salt. If the stems of the chard are tough, remove them entirely from the leaves and discard. (If the stems are tender, simply cut the stems off at the base of the leaves and discard.) Wash the leaves thoroughly. Immerse the chard in the boiling water and cook for 3 minutes *exactly* from the moment you get all the leaves in the pot. Drain immediately but don't squeeze out the liquid.

Warm 3 tablespoons of olive oil in a large (12-inch) sauté pan. Add the sliced garlic and cook over medium heat for 30 seconds. Add the chard, sprinkle with 1 teaspoon salt and ½ teaspoon pepper, and sauté for 3 minutes, tossing frequently with tongs.

Meanwhile, toast or grill 8 slices of bread. When they're nicely browned, rub one side of each slice of bread with a cut side of the halved garlic. Place 2 slices of toasted bread on each plate, garlic side up, and use tongs to distribute the chard onto the toasts. Sprinkle each serving with lemon zest, a squeeze of lemon juice, grated Parmesan cheese, and some fleur de sel. Drizzle the bruschetta with olive oil and serve warm. The liquid from the greens will be absorbed into the bread.

MAKE IT AHEAD: Sauté the chard, cover, and refrigerate in the pan for up to 24 hours. Before serving, reheat the chard, toast the bread, and assemble the bruschettas.

Homemade Chicken Stock makes 6 quarts

I have to include this recipe in every book because it's the basis for so many of my dishes. Of course, you can use canned stock or broth, but this is easy to make and the difference it makes in the finished dish is astonishing. When I'm at home, I throw everything into a big pot and let it simmer away. Four hours later I have quarts of chicken stock to store in the freezer and the house smells wonderful.

3 (5-pound) roasting chickens
3 large yellow onions, unpeeled and quartered
6 carrots, unpeeled and halved crosswise
4 celery stalks with leaves, cut into thirds crosswise
4 parsnips, unpeeled and halved crosswise
20 sprigs fresh flat-leaf parsley
15 sprigs fresh thyme
20 sprigs fresh dill
1 head garlic, unpeeled and cut in half crosswise
2 tablespoons kosher salt
2 teaspoons whole black peppercorns (not ground)

Place the chickens, onions, carrots, celery, parsnips, parsley, thyme, dill, garlic, salt, and peppercorns in a 16- to 20-quart stockpot. Add 7 quarts of water and bring to a boil. Lower the heat and simmer uncovered for 4 hours, skimming off any foam that comes to the top. Set aside until cool enough to handle. Strain the entire contents of the pot through a colander and discard the solids.

MAKE IT AHEAD: Prepare the stock completely, let cool, then pack in containers, and refrigerate for up to 5 days or freeze for up to 4 months.

lunch

Crunchy Iceberg Salad
with Creamy Blue Cheese

Ham & Leek Empanadas

French Green Bean Salad
with Warm Goat Cheese

Quinoa Tabbouleh with Feta

Winter Slaw

Summer Paella Salad

Tomato Mozzarella Pan Bagnat

Zucchini & Goat Cheese Tart

freeze it ahead

My mother had one of those deep freezers in her kitchen that looked like a giant white whale. As far as I could tell, everything she bought at the grocery store went directly into the freezer, and I never really understood why. Was she afraid of running out of food? Did she think fresh food would spoil? Did she only shop once a month? Fresh meat and fish went in, chopped parsley, extra lemon juice, cakes, leftover bread—you name it, it went in there. The top of my wedding cake sat in that freezer for about thirty years. I generally do just the opposite: Nothing used to go into my freezer, except maybe homemade chicken stock, truffle butter, and some ice cream, because I prefer to cook with fresh ingredients. I keep the basics around the house—pasta, olive oil, canned tomatoes—and just shop for a few fresh ingredients every day, depending on what I feel like cooking.

Working on this book has actually taught me that the freezer can be a great resource—but you have to use it properly. I never want to serve something that *tastes* like it just came out of the freezer. I want it to taste as though I whipped it up in the ten minutes before you arrived. The best things to freeze have liquid in them like soups and stews. All you need to do is pack them in containers, freeze them, then simply defrost and reheat them before dinner. For example, a big pot of Zucchini Basil Soup (page 47) can be cooked completely, cooled, and frozen in pint containers so I can serve a warm bowl of soup for lunch whenever it's cold outside. However, some dishes, like Pastitsio (page 124) or Roasted Vegetable Lasagna (page 127), are better assembled and then frozen unbaked so I can throw them into the oven before lunch or dinner. The freezer is also great for desserts: Vanilla Semifreddo with Raspberry Sauce (page 227) and Coffee Granita (page 191) are actually *served* frozen and even the raspberry sauce for the semifreddo can be made ahead and frozen. None of these dishes suffers for having been made in advance and in fact, when the flavors meld, some of them actually taste *better*.

I also learned both how to prepare food for the freezer and how to defrost it. The key is to make a dish, cool it *completely* to room temperature, and wrap it as tightly as possible before freezing it because air is what causes freezer burn and those annoying ice crystals. Don't forget to label everything with the name of the dish *and* the date! How many times have you taken a block of mystery meat out of the freezer and had no idea what it was—or in what decade it had been frozen? There's really no point in putting something into the freezer unless you actually take it out and use it! The best way to defrost most dishes is to leave them in the refrigerator overnight, until completely thawed.

Large things like a Thanksgiving turkey can take as long as two to three days to defrost completely. How many of us have tried to stuff a turkey, only to find that it was still frozen solid after a day in the fridge and we couldn't even get the giblet bag out. Aaarrggh.

In general, soups freeze well, except some soups with cheese—I'm always wary about freezing those because they can curdle and separate. Dishes wrapped in pastry, such as Ham & Leek Empanadas (page 70) and French Chicken Pot Pies (page 98), freeze well before they're baked because the pastry protects the filling and, in the case of the pot pies, the sauce does, too. The sauce retains the moisture in the dish and protects the proteins from getting freezer burn. Pasta sauces freeze well, which means all you'll need to do is boil the pasta and reheat the sauce for a quick weeknight dinner. The most efficient way to store pasta sauce is in plastic freezer bags: Just push out extra air, lay them sideways in the freezer, and then, after they're frozen, pile them up one on top of the other. Baked cakes and breads freeze well but most icings don't, so I bake cakes, wrap them tight, and then defrost them and ice or glaze them before serving.

The good news is that we have access to so many more fresh, local, seasonal ingredients than my mother ever did. I really do try to cook what's fresh, but now I'm also happy to have a few special things socked away in the freezer so I can whip up a beautiful dinner for guests without breaking a sweat. Knowing which things can be frozen yet still taste freshly prepared can make all the difference in your repertoire.

Crunchy Iceberg Salad with Creamy Blue Cheese SERVES 4

This salad has the simplest ingredients but trust me, the result is divine! I tested it one morning and we couldn't wait to eat it for lunch. All the ingredients can be prepped in advance and assembled before serving.

FOR THE DRESSING

4 ounces Roquefort blue cheese, crumbled

⅔ cup good mayonnaise, such as Hellmann's or Best Foods

⅓ cup plain Greek yogurt

1 tablespoon sherry vinegar

Kosher salt and freshly ground black pepper

FOR THE SALAD

4 tender inside celery stalks, trimmed and sliced crosswise ¼ inch thick

6 radishes, trimmed and sliced into thin rounds

5 scallions, trimmed, white and green parts sliced ¼ inch thick

1 large head iceberg lettuce, wilted outer leaves removed

4 to 6 ounces Roquefort blue cheese, crumbled

Fleur de sel

For the dressing, place 4 ounces of blue cheese in a small bowl and microwave for 15 seconds, until it begins to melt. Place the mayonnaise, yogurt, warm blue cheese, sherry vinegar, ½ teaspoon salt, and ¼ teaspoon pepper in the bowl of a food processor fitted with the steel blade and process until smooth. Set aside or refrigerate until ready to use.

For the salad, combine the celery, radishes, and scallions in a bowl. Slice the whole head of lettuce across to make four ¾-inch-thick round disks and place each on a dinner plate. Spoon the dressing on the lettuce and sprinkle on a quarter of the vegetable mixture. Distribute the remaining crumbled blue cheese on the salads, sprinkle with fleur de sel and pepper, and serve.

MAKE IT AHEAD: Prepare the dressing, combine the celery, radishes, and scallions, cover, and refrigerate separately. When ready to serve, slice the lettuce and assemble the salads.

Ham & Leek Empanadas Makes 12

When I was in San Francisco, I stopped at a food truck that made all kinds of empanadas, which inspired this recipe. Instead of making a pastry crust, I use frozen puff pastry, which is so much easier and just as delicious.

1½ tablespoons unsalted butter
1½ cups small-diced leeks, white and light green parts
⅓ cup crème fraîche
4 ounces (¼-inch-diced) smoked ham, such as Black Forest
4 ounces grated Gruyère cheese
2 ounces fresh baby spinach, coarsely chopped (2 cups)
2 tablespoons julienned fresh basil leaves
½ cup freshly grated Parmesan cheese
Kosher salt and freshly ground black pepper
All-purpose flour
3 sheets frozen puff pastry, defrosted (2 packages)
1 egg beaten with 2 tablespoons milk, for egg wash
Fleur de sel or sea salt

When buying the ham, ask to have it sliced ¼ inch thick so you can cut it in ¼-inch dice.

Preheat the oven to 400 degrees. Line 2 sheet pans with parchment paper.

Melt the butter over medium-low heat in a medium (10-inch) sauté pan. Add the leeks and sauté for 4 minutes, until tender but not browned. Stir in the crème fraîche and simmer for a minute.

Combine the ham and Gruyère in a medium bowl. Add the leek mixture, then the spinach, basil, Parmesan, 1¼ teaspoons salt, and ½ teaspoon pepper. Mix and set aside.

Sprinkle a cutting board with flour, roll out one sheet of pastry to an 11 × 11-inch square, and cut it into 4 equal squares. Brush the edge of each square with the egg wash and place ⅓ cup of the filling in the middle. Fold the square diagonally to make a triangle, lining up the edges of the pastry. Place the triangles on the prepared sheet pans and press the edges with the tines of a fork to seal. Brush the triangles with the egg wash and sprinkle with fleur de sel and pepper. Repeat with the remaining pastry and filling. Bake for 20 to 25 minutes, until puffed and golden brown. Allow to cool for 5 minutes and serve hot.

MAKE IT AHEAD: Make and fill the empanadas, wrap tightly, and refrigerate for up to 3 days or freeze for up to 3 months. Brush with egg wash and bake directly from the refrigerator or freezer before serving.

French Green Bean Salad
with Warm Goat Cheese SERVES 4

When I'm in Paris, I love to have a big salad with warm goat cheese for lunch. By wrapping the cheese in phyllo dough and baking it, I end up with a delicious package that's crispy on the outside with creamy goat cheese inside. A cold salad with French string beans is the perfect counterpoint.

12 to 16 ounces Bûcheron goat cheese
8 (8½ × 14-inch) sheets frozen phyllo dough, defrosted
4 tablespoons (½ stick) unsalted butter, melted
Plain dry bread crumbs
Kosher salt and freshly ground black pepper
¾ pound French string beans, trimmed
½ cup good olive oil, at room temperature
1½ tablespoons white wine vinegar
1½ tablespoons Dijon mustard
3 tablespoons minced shallots (2 shallots)
2 tablespoons minced fresh dill
8 ounces mesclun mix or salad greens

French string beans are also called haricots verts.

I use Athens phyllo dough.

Preheat the oven to 375 degrees.

Score the goat cheese rind at ½-inch intervals and make 4 slices by pulling dental floss through the log. Place the stack of phyllo dough sheets on a cutting board and cover it with a slightly damp towel. Place one sheet of phyllo on the board, brush it with butter, and sprinkle it with ¾ teaspoon of bread crumbs. Place a second sheet of phyllo on top, brush it with butter, and sprinkle it with bread crumbs, continuing until you have 4 sheets of phyllo stacked up. Cut the phyllo in half crosswise to make two (7 × 8½-inch) rectangles.

Place a slice of goat cheese in the middle of one stack of phyllo, fold a corner diagonally over the cheese, and pleat the rest of the dough up and around the cheese, enclosing it completely. Place the package, folded side up, on a sheet pan lined with parchment paper. Repeat the process, until you have 4 packages filled

MAKE IT AHEAD: Assemble the goat cheese packages, cook the beans, and prepare the salad and vinaigrette; refrigerate separately for up to 2 days. Before serving, bake the cheese packages, combine the salad and vinaigrette, and serve.

with goat cheese. Brush the packages all over with melted butter, cover, and refrigerate until ready to bake.

Bring a large pot of salted water to a boil and add the string beans. Simmer for exactly 3 minutes, until crisp-tender. Drain immediately and immerse the beans in ice water to stop the cooking. Drain well.

For the vinaigrette, whisk together the olive oil, vinegar, mustard, shallots, 1 teaspoon salt, and ½ teaspoon pepper. Stir in the dill and set aside.

Bake the goat cheese packages for 15 to 20 minutes, until golden brown. Toss the string beans and mesclun with enough dressing to moisten. Divide the salad among 4 lunch plates, top each with a warm goat cheese package, and serve immediately.

Quinoa Tabbouleh with Feta SERVES 8

Quinoa is a grain that originated in South America and is considered a "superfood" because it has more protein than most grains. It also has a wonderful nutty flavor. I decided to use quinoa instead of bulghur in my favorite tabbouleh and found it to be even more delicious. Feta, scallions, mint, and parsley give this dish lots of flavor.

1 cup quinoa
Kosher salt and freshly ground black pepper
¼ cup freshly squeezed lemon juice (2 lemons)
¼ cup good olive oil
1 cup thinly sliced scallions, white and green parts
   (5 scallions)
1 cup chopped fresh mint leaves (2 bunches)
1 cup chopped fresh flat-leaf parsley
1 hothouse cucumber, unpeeled, seeded, and
   medium-diced
2 cups cherry tomatoes, halved through the stem
2 cups medium-diced feta (8 ounces)

Pour 2 cups of water into a medium saucepan and bring to a boil. Add the quinoa and 1 teaspoon of salt, lower the heat, and simmer covered for 15 minutes, until the grains are tender and open (they'll have little curly tails). Drain, place in a bowl, and immediately add the lemon juice, olive oil, and 1½ teaspoons of salt.

In a large bowl, combine the scallions, mint, parsley, cucumber, tomatoes, 2 teaspoons salt, and 1 teaspoon pepper. Add the quinoa and mix well. Carefully fold in the feta and taste for seasonings. Serve at room temperature or refrigerate and serve cold.

MAKE IT AHEAD: Prepare the salad without the feta, cover, and refrigerate for up to 4 days. Fold in the feta and serve.

Winter Slaw SERVES 8

Kale is so popular now that happily, it's available in grocery stores everywhere. Most markets carry both curly and flat varieties, but for this recipe I prefer the curly kind. Winter slaw is like coleslaw but with kale, Brussels sprouts, and radicchio instead of cabbage. I like it with a lemon vinaigrette and big shavings of Parmesan cheese.

½ pound large kale leaves, center rib removed (6 to 8 leaves)
6 ounces Brussels sprouts, trimmed, halved, and cored
½ small head radicchio, cored
¼ cup freshly squeezed lemon juice (2 lemons)
½ cup good olive oil
Kosher salt and freshly ground black pepper
1 (6-ounce) chunk good Parmesan cheese
1 cup dried cranberries

With a very sharp chef's knife, cut the kale, Brussels sprouts, and radicchio crosswise in thin shreds, as you would cut cabbage for coleslaw, and place them in a large bowl.

In a small bowl or liquid measuring cup, whisk together the lemon juice, olive oil, 1 teaspoon salt, and ½ teaspoon pepper. Pour enough dressing on the salad to just moisten it, reserving the rest.

Shave the Parmesan in big shards with a vegetable peeler. Add the cheese and dried cranberries to the salad and toss it carefully to avoid breaking up the cheese. Check for seasonings, add more vinaigrette, if necessary, and serve cold or at room temperature.

MAKE IT AHEAD: Prepare the salad ingredients, store in plastic bags, and refrigerate for a day or two. Make the vinaigrette and refrigerate for up to one day. Toss together a few hours before serving.

Summer Paella Salad SERVES 6 TO 7

Paella is great for parties because it's dinner in one dish. Instead of a hot dinner, this is a cold version with similar ingredients—saffron rice, chicken, shrimp, mussels, and lots of spicy sausage. I serve this with a glass of Summer Rosé Sangria (page 24).

16- to 20-count shrimp refers to the number of shrimp in a pound. Always order it by the count rather than the terms jumbo or large.

4 cups good chicken stock, preferably homemade (page 62)

1 teaspoon dried fennel seeds

½ teaspoon curry powder

½ teaspoon saffron threads

½ teaspoon crushed red pepper flakes

Kosher salt and freshly ground black pepper

3 tablespoons good olive oil

1½ cups chopped red onion (1 large)

1 tablespoon minced garlic (3 cloves)

1½ cups long-grain white rice, such as Carolina

2 boneless, skinless chicken breasts, 1-inch-diced

1 pound (16- to 20-count) shrimp, peeled and deveined (see note)

1 cup (½-inch-diced) celery

1 cup sliced scallions, white and green parts (5 scallions)

1 cup frozen peas, such as Birds Eye Garden Peas

1 Holland red bell pepper, cored, seeded, and ¾-inch-diced

1 Holland yellow bell pepper, cored, seeded, and ¾-inch-diced

8 ounces kielbasa, sliced diagonally ¼ inch thick

¾ cup pitted Kalamata olives

½ cup freshly squeezed lemon juice (3 lemons)

½ pound mussels, scrubbed and debearded

Combine the chicken stock, fennel seeds, curry powder, saffron, red pepper flakes, 1 tablespoon salt, and 1 teaspoon black pepper in a large saucepan, bring to a simmer, remove from the heat, and set aside.

MAKE IT AHEAD: Prepare the salad completely, cover, and refrigerate for up to 3 days.

Heat the olive oil in a medium (10-inch) Dutch oven, such as Le Creuset, add the onion, and cook over medium heat for 5 minutes, until tender. Add the garlic and cook for one minute. Stir in the rice and cook for 2 minutes. Stir in the stock mixture, bring to a boil, lower the heat, and simmer covered for 10 minutes. Stir in the chicken, cover, and cook for 10 minutes. Stir in the shrimp, cover, and simmer for 5 minutes, until the shrimp are barely cooked and the rice is almost tender. Turn off the heat, cover, and allow to sit for 15 minutes.

Meanwhile, in a very large bowl, combine the celery, scallions, peas, red peppers, yellow peppers, kielbasa, and olives. Stir in the warm rice mixture and the lemon juice and set aside to cool. Boil ½ cup water in a medium saucepan, add the mussels, cover, and simmer for 4 to 5 minutes, until the mussels open. Add the mussels to the salad. Cover the salad and allow it to sit at room temperature for about an hour to allow the flavors to blend. Taste for seasonings and serve at room temperature.

Tomato Mozzarella Pan Bagnat

MAKES 4 SANDWICHES

Pan bagnat is a classic Provençal sandwich with tomatoes, tuna, and lots of flavors of the Mediterranean—capers, olives, anchovies, garlic, and basil. This is my vegetarian twist on that sandwich.

3 tablespoons minced shallots (2 shallots)
2 teaspoons minced garlic (2 cloves)
1½ tablespoons red wine vinegar
1 tablespoon balsamic vinegar
2 teaspoons Dijon mustard
Kosher salt and freshly ground black pepper
½ cup good olive oil
6 anchovy fillets, drained and minced (optional)
2 tablespoons drained capers
¼ cup Kalamata olives, pitted and chopped
2 medium ripe tomatoes
4 individual ciabatta rolls, cut in half horizontally
6 to 8 ounces lightly salted fresh mozzarella, thinly sliced
½ cup julienned fresh basil leaves

For the vinaigrette, whisk the shallots, garlic, red wine vinegar, balsamic vinegar, mustard, 2 teaspoons salt, and 1 teaspoon pepper together in a small bowl. Slowly whisk in the olive oil, stir in the anchovies (if using), capers, and olives, and set aside.

Core the tomatoes and slice them ⅓ inch thick. Place the bottom halves of the ciabattas, cut side up, on a sheet pan. Place a layer of tomato on each bread, spoon on ⅔ of the vinaigrette, add a layer of mozzarella, and sprinkle with the basil leaves. Spoon the remaining vinaigrette on the cut sides of the ciabatta tops and place them, cut side down, on the sandwiches. Place a second sheet pan on the sandwiches and put weights on top, such as cans of tomatoes. Allow the sandwiches to sit at room temperature for an hour for the flavors to blend.

Heat an electric panini press and toast the sandwiches for 5 to 10 minutes, until the bread is toasted and the mozzarella starts to melt. Cut each sandwich in half and serve warm.

MAKE IT AHEAD: Assemble the sandwiches, wrap, and refrigerate for up to a day. Toast before serving.

Zucchini & Goat Cheese Tart serves 6

Maria and Robert Sinskey own Robert Sinskey Vineyards in Napa, California. Robert runs the vineyard and Maria cooks extraordinary meals for visitors. She made this amazing tart for us; her tip is that a drop of vinegar in the crust makes it flaky!

1¼ cups all-purpose flour

Kosher salt and freshly ground black pepper

10 tablespoons (1¼ sticks) cold unsalted butter, ½-inch-diced

½ teaspoon white wine vinegar

5 tablespoons ice water

1½ pounds zucchini, unpeeled and sliced ⅛ inch thick (see note)

2 tablespoons good olive oil, divided

8 ounces plain creamy goat cheese, such as Montrachet, at room temperature

1 teaspoon minced fresh thyme leaves

¼ teaspoon grated lemon zest

Choose zucchini that have similar diameters so the slices will be uniform. Slice by hand or with a mandoline.

Place the flour, ¾ teaspoon of salt, and the butter in the bowl of a food processor fitted with the steel blade and pulse 12 to 14 times, until the butter is the size of peas. With the processor running, pour the vinegar and ice water through the feed tube and continue to process and pulse until the dough just comes together. Dump out on a floured board, form into a disk, wrap in plastic, and chill for 30 minutes.

Meanwhile, place the zucchini in a colander set over a plate. Toss it with 2 teaspoons of salt and set aside for 30 minutes. Spread the zucchini out on a clean dish towel, roll it up, and squeeze gently to remove some of the liquid. Put the zucchini slices into a bowl and toss with 1 tablespoon of olive oil. With a fork, mash together the goat cheese, thyme, lemon zest, ½ teaspoon salt, and ¼ teaspoon pepper and set aside.

MAKE IT AHEAD: Roll out the dough and assemble the tart. Cover, and refrigerate for up to 4 hours. Bake before serving.

To make an 11-inch circle, roll the dough to 12 or 13 inches in diameter, fold it in quarters, and trim the edge with a sharp knife. When you unfold the pastry, it will be a circle.

Preheat the oven to 400 degrees. Roll the dough out on a floured board to an 11-inch circle (see note) and place on a sheet pan lined with parchment paper. Spread the dough with the goat cheese mixture, leaving a ½-inch border. Lay the zucchini slices in tightly overlapping circles, starting at the very edge of the pastry (the zucchini will shrink when it bakes). Continue overlapping circles of zucchini until the whole tart is covered. Drizzle with the remaining tablespoon of olive oil and sprinkle with pepper. Bake for 40 to 50 minutes, until the dough is golden brown. Cut in wedges and serve hot, warm, or at room temperature.

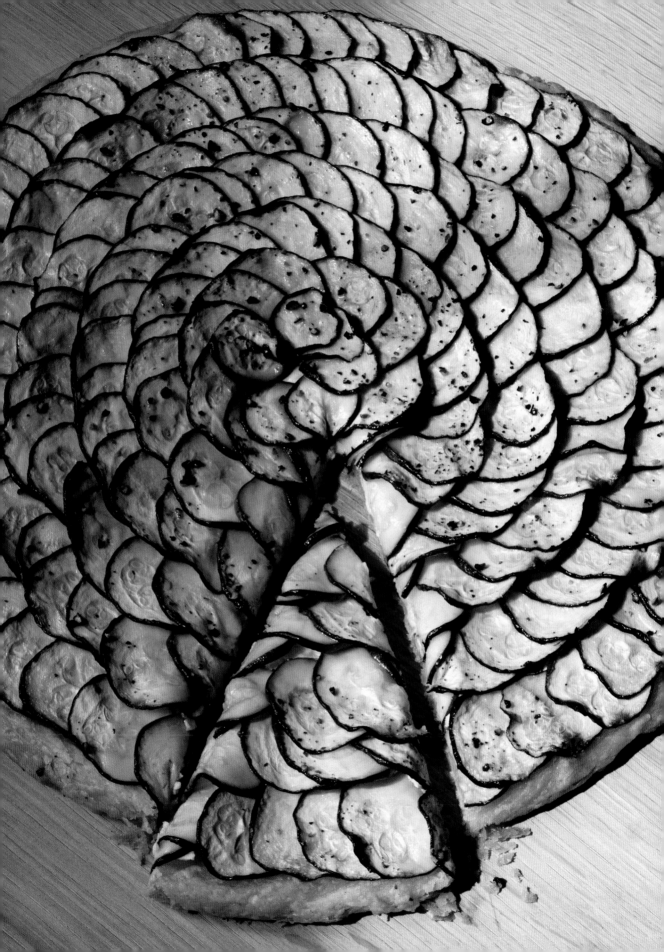

dinner

Roast Chicken
with Bread & Arugula Salad

French Chicken Pot Pies

Make-Ahead Roast Turkey

Make-Ahead Turkey Gravy
with Onions & Sage

Slow-Roasted Spiced Pork

Herbed Pork Tenderloins
with Apple Chutney

Moroccan Lamb Tagine

Summer Filet of Beef
with Béarnaise Mayonnaise

Grilled New York Strip Steaks

Rosemary Rack of Lamb
with Easy Tzatziki

Pastitsio

Roasted Vegetable Lasagna

Herb-Roasted Fish

Easy Coquilles Saint Jacques

Provençal Fish Stew
with Sriracha Rouille

Garlic & Herb Roasted
Shrimp

make-ahead thanksgiving

I love Thanksgiving! There are so many traditional dishes that I can't wait to make. I invite my dearest friends to come with their children and grandchildren and we have a wonderful day together. I don't make it easy on myself, though; not only do I make Thanksgiving dinner for all of us, but every year I make enough so my guests can take leftovers home. Isn't that the best part of Thanksgiving—turkey and stuffing sandwiches for lunch the next day?! Every year, I panic as Thanksgiving approaches, wondering how in the world I will get all those dishes—soup, turkey, stuffing, lots of vegetables and desserts—cooked at the same time.

This year I was determined to figure out how I could enjoy my favorite meal instead of letting it totally stress me out. A week before Thanksgiving, I created a menu entirely of dishes that could be assembled or cooked completely ahead of time, including the turkey! Then I wrote two schedules. The first one outlined when I would make each dish. I cooked or prepped two or three dishes a day, starting on Monday with Warm Fig & Arugula Salad (page 50) and Carrot & Cauliflower Purée (page 169). On Tuesday, I seasoned the Make-Ahead Roast Turkey (page 101), prepared the Make-Ahead Turkey Gravy (page 103), cut the Brussels sprouts for roasting, and stored them all in the refrigerator. On Wednesday, I assembled the Baked Farro & Butternut Squash (page 173) and the Leek & Artichoke Bread Pudding (page 178), which could all just sit in the refrigerator until I was ready to bake them before dinner on Thursday. I also prepared the Make-Ahead Zabaglione with Amaretti (page 225) to have on hand as an extra dessert (I asked my guests to bring their favorite pies).

The second schedule I made was for the ovens on Thanksgiving Day: Oven #1 was for the Make-Ahead Roast Turkey, early in the day. I roasted it and carved it onto an ovenproof platter with gravy, which I could reheat later. An hour before dinner, I baked the Leek & Artichoke Bread Pudding, which I had assembled in advance. In oven #2, I made the Baked Farro & Butternut Squash and the Roasted Brussels Sprouts from *The Barefoot Contessa Cookbook*. On top of the stove, I reheated extra Make-Ahead Turkey Gravy and the Carrot & Cauliflower Purée. If you only have one oven, planning is even more important! I would choose side dishes that all bake at almost the same temperature so they can roast or be reheated together—or sides that you can reheat on the stovetop. Remember that many dishes can be kept warm under a tent of aluminum foil while the rest of them are reheating in the oven!

With a little bit of planning, everything fit together perfectly, and I was able to get a delicious dinner to the table with less stress than any other year. This was truly my dream Thanksgiving dinner!

Roast Chicken with Bread & Arugula Salad SERVES 4

You'd think that after roasting chickens for forty-five years, I would have nothing more to learn—but of course, there always is! This incredibly delicious roast chicken is inspired by Zuni Café in San Francisco and Standard Grill in New York City. This is particularly my homage to the late Judy Rodgers, of Zuni Café, who was so beloved and taught us all about rustic country food.

1 (4- to 4½-pound) whole chicken, preferably Bell & Evans
4 sprigs fresh thyme
2 large garlic cloves, smashed flat
1 lemon, quartered
2 teaspoons fine sea salt, plus extra for serving
½ teaspoon freshly ground black pepper
3 to 4 (¾-inch-thick) slices country bread
Good olive oil
Arugula Salad (recipe follows)

Place the chicken in a baking dish. Using your fingers, gently loosen the skin from the breasts and thighs without breaking the skin. Carefully slide the sprigs of thyme and the garlic under the skin. Put the lemon in the cavity. Tie the legs together and tuck the wings under the body. Sprinkle with 2 teaspoons of sea salt and the pepper, cover the dish tightly with plastic wrap, and refrigerate for 24 to 48 hours.

Preheat the oven to 500 degrees. (Be sure your oven is very clean!) Place the bread in a medium (10-inch) cast-iron skillet in a single layer. Brush the chicken with olive oil and place it, breast side up, on top of the bread. Roast for 30 minutes, turn it over and roast for 15 minutes, until the juices run clear when you cut between the leg and the thigh. Wrap the skillet tightly with aluminum foil and allow the chicken to rest at room temperature for a full 30 minutes. (Don't worry; it will stay hot.) The bread will be almost burnt on the bottom and soft with the pan drippings on top.

MAKE IT AHEAD: Season the chicken. Up to a day ahead, clean the arugula, prepare the vinaigrette, and refrigerate separately. Roast the chicken and assemble the salad before serving.

To carve, cut off the legs and cut between the thigh and the leg. For the breasts, cut the wings off, remove each breast in one large piece, and make thick slices crosswise.

Place the Arugula Salad in a very large, shallow serving platter. Put the chicken and the bread on a cutting board. Cut the bread into 1-inch squares and sprinkle them on the salad. Carve the chicken thickly (see note) and place it on top of the salad. Spoon the pan juices over the chicken, sprinkle it with sea salt, and serve warm.

Arugula Salad SERVES 4

Baby arugula holds up better than traditional arugula under the warm chicken.

¼ cup Champagne vinegar
1 teaspoon Dijon mustard
1 teaspoon minced garlic
Kosher salt and freshly ground black pepper
½ cup good olive oil
½ cup thinly sliced scallions, white and green parts (3 scallions)
2 tablespoons dried currants
6 cups baby arugula, lightly packed (6 to 8 ounces)

Whisk the vinegar, mustard, garlic, 1 teaspoon salt, and ½ teaspoon pepper together in a small bowl or glass measuring cup. Whisk in the olive oil, stir in the scallions and currants, and set aside.

Place the arugula in a large bowl, add the vinaigrette, and toss well.

French Chicken Pot Pies makes 6 servings

*I believe in mastering one recipe and then making variations. This is
a twist on a classic American pot pie but dressed up for company. It has
French ingredients like leeks and tarragon, and I use puff pastry to make
the crust easy!*

*The egg wash both affixes the
pastry to the dish and makes a
lovely browned crust.*

4 split (2 whole) chicken breasts, bone-in and skin-on
  (2½ pounds)
Good olive oil
Kosher salt and freshly ground black pepper
6 tablespoons (¾ stick) unsalted butter
4 cups chopped leeks, white and light green parts (4 leeks)
2 cups (½-inch-diced) carrots (5 carrots)
4 teaspoons minced garlic (4 cloves)
8 ounces cremini mushrooms, stems discarded; sliced
¼ cup minced fresh tarragon leaves
⅓ cup all-purpose flour
2½ cups good chicken stock, preferably homemade
  (page 62)
6 tablespoons cream sherry
½ cup heavy cream
1 (10-ounce) package frozen peas, such as Birds Eye
  Garden Peas
3 sheets frozen puff pastry, such as Pepperidge Farm
  (2 boxes), defrosted
1 extra-large egg beaten with 1 tablespoon water, for
  egg wash
Fleur de sel

Preheat the oven to 350 degrees.

Pat the chicken dry with paper towels, place on a sheet pan, brush with olive oil, and sprinkle with salt and pepper. Roast for 35 minutes, until cooked through. Set aside until cool enough to handle. Discard the skin and bones and cut the meat in ¾-inch dice. You should have about 5 cups of chicken.

Meanwhile, heat the butter in a medium heavy-bottomed pot or Dutch oven, such as Le Creuset. Add the leeks and carrots and

MAKE IT AHEAD: Assemble
the pot pies completely, cover
tightly, and refrigerate for
up to a day or freeze for up
to a month. Defrost overnight
in the refrigerator (if frozen)
and bake before serving.

sauté over medium-high heat for 8 to 10 minutes, until they begin to soften. Add the garlic, mushrooms, and tarragon and cook for 5 minutes. Sprinkle on the flour and cook for 30 seconds, stirring constantly. Add the chicken stock and sherry, bring to a boil, then lower the heat and simmer for 2 minutes, until the mixture is slightly thickened. Add the cream, 2 teaspoons salt, and 1 teaspoon pepper and simmer for 5 minutes. Stir in the frozen peas and chicken, taste for seasonings, and pour the mixture into six (2-cup) ovenproof serving bowls.

Raise the oven to 400 degrees.

On a lightly floured board, roll each pastry to an 11-inch square. Cut out 2 circles from each sheet of pastry that are each ½ inch larger than the rim of the bowl. Brush the outer edges of the bowls with the egg wash. Place a pastry circle over each bowl, adhering it with the egg wash. Brush the pastry with egg wash and sprinkle with fleur de sel and pepper. Make three 1-inch slits in each pastry for steam to escape. Refrigerate the pot pies for at least 30 minutes. Place on a sheet pan lined with parchment paper and bake for 30 to 40 minutes, until the crust is golden brown and the filling is bubbly. Serve hot.

Make-Ahead Roast Turkey serves 8

The most stressful things about Thanksgiving are carving the turkey at
the last minute and keeping it hot on the buffet. What I discovered is that I
could carve the turkey in advance, arrange it on an ovenproof platter over
a layer of gravy, and then reheat it all together. Not only was the turkey
moist and delicious, but it stayed hot longer!

Kosher salt and freshly ground black pepper
1 tablespoon minced fresh thyme leaves
Grated zest of 1 lemon
1 (12- to 14-pound) fresh turkey
1 large yellow onion, unpeeled and cut in eighths
1 lemon, quartered
8 sprigs fresh thyme
4 tablespoons (½ stick) unsalted butter, melted
Make-Ahead Turkey Gravy (page 103)

Two or three days before you plan to roast the turkey, combine
3 tablespoons of salt, the minced thyme, and lemon zest. Wash
the turkey inside and out, drain it well, and pat it all over with
paper towels. Sprinkle 1 tablespoon of the salt mixture in the
cavity of the turkey and rub the rest on the skin, including under
the wings and legs. Place the turkey in a shallow dish just large
enough to hold it and wrap it tightly with plastic wrap. Refrigerate for one or two days. The day before you plan to roast the
turkey, remove the plastic wrap and leave the turkey in the fridge.
The skin will dry out and turn a little translucent.

Preheat the oven to 325 degrees. Put the turkey in a large
roasting pan, discarding any juices in the dish. Place the onion,
lemon, and thyme sprigs in the cavity. With kitchen string, tie the
legs together and the wings close to the body. Brush the turkey
with the butter and sprinkle it generously with salt and pepper.

Roast the turkey for 2 to 2¼ hours, until the breast meat
registers 165 degrees (put the thermometer in sideways) on an
instant-read thermometer. Remove from the oven and place the
turkey on a platter. Cut off the legs and thighs and put them back
into the roasting pan, covering the breast and carcass tightly with

MAKE IT AHEAD: Roast and
slice the turkey and assemble it
on the gravy. Cover and allow
to sit at room temperature
for up to 1 hour before reheating
in the oven.

aluminum foil. Place the roasting pan back in the oven for 15 to 20 minutes, until the dark meat registers 180 degrees. Remove the dark meat to the platter with the turkey, cover it tightly with aluminum foil, and allow it to rest at room temperature for 15 minutes.

Pour a ¼-inch layer of the gravy into a large (12 × 16-inch), ovenproof serving platter (make sure it's ovenproof!). Carve the turkey and arrange it artfully on top of the gravy. Place the platter uncovered into the oven for 15 to 30 minutes, until the turkey is very hot. Serve hot with extra gravy on the side.

Make-Ahead Turkey Gravy with Onions & Sage MAKES 4 CUPS

No one wants to stand around hoping their gravy won't be lumpy at the moment the turkey comes out of the oven. With this recipe, that will never happen! The gravy base can be simmered up to a week ahead with onions, sage, and Cognac and whisked into the pan after the turkey is done.

6 tablespoons (¾ stick) unsalted butter

1 large red onion, halved and sliced ¼ inch thick

4 large garlic cloves, peeled and halved

6 tablespoons all-purpose flour

4 cups good chicken stock, preferably homemade (page 62)

2 tablespoons Cognac or brandy

10 large fresh sage leaves

2 bay leaves

Kosher salt and freshly ground black pepper

1 cup dry white wine, such as Pinot Grigio

Melt the butter in a large saucepan over medium heat. Add the onion and garlic and sauté, stirring often, for 15 to 20 minutes, until the onion becomes browned and starts to caramelize. Sprinkle on the flour and cook, stirring constantly, for 1½ minutes. Stir in the chicken stock, Cognac, sage leaves, bay leaves, 2 teaspoons salt (depending on the saltiness of the chicken stock), and 1 teaspoon pepper. Bring to a boil, lower the heat, and simmer for 20 minutes, stirring occasionally. Set aside at room temperature for 1 hour and strain, pressing the solids lightly and then discarding them. Refrigerate until ready to use.

After the turkey is cooked, remove it to a carving board to rest while you finish the gravy. Place the roasting pan on the stovetop over medium heat and add the wine. Bring to a boil, lower the heat, and simmer for 2 minutes, stirring and scraping up all the bits clinging to the bottom of the pan. Slowly whisk the gravy base into the pan. Simmer for about 5 minutes, until the gravy is smooth and slightly thickened. Taste for seasonings and serve hot.

MAKE IT AHEAD: Make the gravy base and refrigerate for up to a week or freeze for up to 3 months.

Slow-Roasted Spiced Pork

SERVES 8 TO 10

This has become my favorite dish for winter entertaining. I rub the pork with the seasoning mixture in advance and then just throw it in the oven to roast for 6 to 7 hours before dinner. My favorite accompaniments are Maple Baked Beans (Barefoot Contessa at Home) and Winter Slaw (page 77).

1 (7- to 9-pound) bone-in pork butt with a layer of fat on top
6 garlic cloves
1 large yellow onion, chopped
1 jalapeño pepper, ribs removed, seeded, and chopped
¼ cup chopped fresh oregano leaves
1½ tablespoons ground cumin
1½ teaspoons chipotle chile powder
Kosher salt and freshly ground black pepper
1½ tablespoons apple cider vinegar
¼ cup good olive oil
1 (750 ml) bottle dry white wine, such as Pinot Grigio
Limes wedges, for serving

Preheat the oven to 300 degrees. Test your oven with an oven thermometer to be sure it's accurate!

Score the fat on the pork diagonally with a sharp knife in a crosshatch pattern. With a small paring knife, make a dozen ½-inch-deep cuts in the top and sides of the pork to allow the seasonings to permeate the meat.

Place the garlic, onion, jalapeño, and oregano in a food processor and process until the ingredients are finely chopped. Add the cumin, chile powder, 1 tablespoon salt, and 1½ tea-spoons pepper and process for 30 seconds to make a paste. Add the vinegar and olive oil and process to incorporate. Rub the mixture all over the pork, including the sides and the bottom, and place the pork in a large roasting pan, fat side up. Pour 2 cups of the wine into the pan and cover the whole roasting pan tightly with aluminum foil. Roast for 2½ hours, remove the foil, and roast for another 4 to 4½ hours, until the meat is very, very tender when tested with a carving fork. Every 2 hours, add another cup of wine to keep some liquid in the pan.

MAKE IT AHEAD: Make the paste, rub on the pork, and refrigerate for up to 24 hours. Roast before dinner.

Remove the pan from the oven, cover it tightly with aluminum foil, and allow the meat to rest for 15 to 30 minutes. Slice, sprinkle with salt, and serve with lime wedges on the side.

To make corn bread squares, prepare the Sour Cream Corn Bread (page 239) batter, pour it into a 9 × 13-inch baking pan, and bake at 350 degrees for 25 minutes, until a toothpick comes out clean.

Herbed Pork Tenderloins with Apple Chutney

SERVES 6 TO 8

Cooking pork tenderloins for the first time was a revelation to me because I didn't grow up eating pork. I prep them—seasoning them with rosemary and thyme and wrapping them with prosciutto—and then roast them just before dinner. I love to serve these with homemade apple chutney.

2 pork tenderloins (2½ to 3 pounds total)
1 tablespoon minced fresh rosemary leaves
1 tablespoon chopped fresh thyme leaves
Kosher salt and freshly ground black pepper
Good olive oil
10 to 12 slices prosciutto
Apple Chutney (page 113)

Pork can be cooked medium rare because there is no longer a concern about trichinosis. Overcooked pork will be dry and flavorless.

Preheat the oven to 450 degrees.

Place the tenderloins on a sheet pan and pat them dry with paper towels. Combine the rosemary, thyme, 1 tablespoon salt, and 1 teaspoon pepper in a small bowl. Rub the tenderloins all over with 2 tablespoons of olive oil. Sprinkle all sides with the herb mixture. If there is a thinner "tail," fold it underneath so the tenderloin is an even thickness throughout. Wrap the tenderloins completely with a single layer of prosciutto. (I place the prosciutto sideways with the ends wrapping under the tenderloins.) Tie in several places with kitchen string to hold the prosciutto and the "tail" in place.

Roast for 20 to 25 minutes, until an instant-read thermometer inserted in the middle of the end of the tenderloin reads 140 degrees for medium rare and 145 degrees for medium. Cover the tenderloins tightly with aluminum foil and allow to rest at room temperature for 15 minutes. Slice diagonally in thick slices and serve warm with the Apple Chutney.

MAKE IT AHEAD: Assemble the pork completely, wrap tightly, and refrigerate for up to 24 hours. Roast before serving.

Moroccan Lamb Tagine serves 6

There's a wonderful cookbook from Australia by Bill Granger called Bill's
Sydney Food. *This tagine is inspired by one of his recipes. The flavors are
nuanced and complex but there's not one ingredient you can't find in the
grocery store.*

Good olive oil
6 small frenched lamb shanks (5 to 6 pounds total) (see note)
3 cups chopped yellow onions (2 large onions)
3 garlic cloves, thinly sliced
1 tablespoon grated fresh ginger
1½ teaspoons chili powder
1½ teaspoons ground turmeric
1½ teaspoons ground cumin
½ teaspoon ground cardamom
1 (4-inch) cinnamon stick
1 (28-ounce) can diced tomatoes, such as San Marzano
   (see note)
2 cups good chicken stock, preferably homemade (page 62)
2 tablespoons light brown sugar, lightly packed
4 (½-inch-thick) slices of lime
Kosher salt and freshly ground black pepper
1 pound Yukon Gold potatoes, unpeeled and 1-inch-diced
1 pound butternut squash, peeled and 1-inch-diced
½ pound sweet potatoes, unpeeled and 1-inch-diced
Steamed Couscous (recipe follows), for serving

*If you can't find diced San
Marzano tomatoes, pour a can of
whole peeled tomatoes, with the
liquid, into a food processor fitted
with the steel blade and process
until the tomatoes are chopped.*

Preheat the oven to 300 degrees.

Heat 2 tablespoons of olive oil in a very large (12- to 13-inch)
pot or Dutch oven, such as Le Creuset. Pat the lamb shanks dry
with paper towels. In batches, add the lamb shanks to the pot
and cook over medium heat for 3 minutes on each side, until they
are nicely browned. Transfer to a plate and brown the remaining shanks, adding a little more oil, if necessary. Transfer all the
shanks to the plate and set aside.

MAKE IT AHEAD: Assemble
completely, refrigerate, and bake
before serving.

Ask your butcher for small lamb shanks, which are from the front legs, rather than the large rear ones.

Add the onions and cook over medium-low heat for 5 minutes, stirring occasionally, adding more oil, if necessary. Add the garlic and ginger and cook for just 30 seconds. Add the chili powder, turmeric, cumin, cardamom, and cinnamon and cook for one minute. Stir in the tomatoes and their liquid, the chicken stock, brown sugar, lime, 1 tablespoon salt, and 1 teaspoon pepper. Add the potatoes, butternut squash, and sweet potatoes and bring to a boil. Place the lamb shanks in the pot, spooning some of the sauce and vegetables over the shanks. (They will not be completely submerged.) Cover the pot and bake for 3 hours, until the lamb shanks are very tender. Serve hot with steamed couscous.

Steamed Couscous SERVES 6

4 tablespoons (½ stick) unsalted butter
2 cups chopped yellow onions (2 onions)
3 cups good chicken stock, preferably homemade (page 62)
Kosher salt and freshly ground black pepper
2 cups couscous (12 ounces)

Melt the butter in a large saucepan. Add the onions and cook over medium heat for 10 minutes, stirring occasionally, until tender but not browned. Add the chicken stock, 1½ teaspoons salt, and ½ teaspoon pepper and bring to a full boil. Stir in the couscous, turn off the heat, cover, and allow to steam for 10 minutes. Fluff with a fork and serve hot.

MAKE IT AHEAD: Cook the onion and stock mixture, cool, and refrigerate. Before serving, reheat, stir in the couscous, turn off the heat, cover, and allow to steam for 10 minutes.

Apple Chutney

MAKES 5 CUPS

Of course, you can serve Herbed Pork Tenderloins (page 109) with store-bought chutney but homemade apple chutney with fresh ginger and raisins is easy to make and delicious!

1 cup chopped yellow onion

2 tablespoons minced or grated fresh ginger (see note)

1 cup freshly squeezed orange juice (4 oranges)

¾ cup apple cider vinegar

1 cup light brown sugar, lightly packed

1 teaspoon whole mustard seeds

¼ teaspoon crushed red pepper flakes

1½ teaspoons kosher salt

6 Granny Smith apples, peeled, cored, and ½-inch-diced

¾ cup raisins

To mince ginger, I peel it, dice it, and process it in a mini food processor.

MAKE IT AHEAD: Store covered in the refrigerator for up to 2 weeks.

Combine the onion, ginger, orange juice, vinegar, brown sugar, mustard seeds, red pepper flakes, and salt in a medium-size saucepan. Add the apples, adding them as you chop to keep them from turning brown. Bring to a boil over medium-high heat, stirring occasionally. Reduce the heat and simmer for 50 minutes to 1 hour, stirring occasionally, until most of the liquid has evaporated. Stir in the raisins and serve warm, at room temperature, or cold.

Summer Filet of Beef with Béarnaise Mayonnaise

I'm endlessly interested in the cookbooks written by Sarah Leah Chase.
Her recipes are for the kind of simple, delicious food I love. This béarnaise
mayonnaise is inspired by a recipe in her Open House Cookbook. *It's a*
great dish to make in the summer because you can roast the beef in advance
and serve it at room temperature with the mayonnaise.

- 1 whole (4- to 5-pound) beef tenderloin, trimmed and tied
- 6 tablespoons (¾ stick) unsalted butter, melted
- Kosher salt and freshly ground black pepper
- ¾ cup minced shallots (3 shallots)
- 4 tablespoons minced fresh tarragon leaves, divided
- ½ cup dry white wine
- ¼ cup tarragon or white wine vinegar
- 2 extra-large egg yolks, at room temperature
- 2 tablespoons freshly squeezed lemon juice, at room temperature
- 1 tablespoon Dijon mustard
- 1 cup vegetable or canola oil, at room temperature
- ½ cup good olive oil, at room temperature

Preheat the oven to 275 degrees. Line a sheet pan with aluminum foil.

Dry the entire tenderloin with paper towels and brush it all over (top and bottom) with the butter. Sprinkle it all over with 4 teaspoons of salt and 2 teaspoons of pepper. It will seem like a lot but trust me, it's important.

Place the filet on the sheet pan and roast it for 1 to 1¼ hours, until an instant-read thermometer inserted into the end of the beef registers 130 degrees for medium rare. Remove from the oven, cover tightly with aluminum foil, and allow to rest at room temperature for 15 minutes. Discard the foil and allow to sit at room temperature.

Meanwhile, place the shallots, 3 tablespoons of tarragon, the wine, and vinegar in a small saucepan and bring it to a boil over

MAKE IT AHEAD: Roast the beef and make the mayonnaise. Wrap both well and refrigerate for up to 2 days.

medium-high heat. Boil for 5 minutes, until only 1 tablespoon of liquid remains. Set aside to cool for 15 minutes.

Place the egg yolks, lemon juice, mustard, 2½ teaspoons salt, and 1 teaspoon pepper in the bowl of a food processor fitted with the steel blade and process for 10 seconds. With the processor running, slowly pour the vegetable oil and olive oil through the feed tube to make a thick emulsion. Add the shallot reduction and the remaining table-spoon of tarragon leaves and pulse to combine. Refrigerate until ready to serve.

Slice the filet of beef between ¼ and ½ inch thick, sprinkle with salt, and serve warm, at room temperature, or cold with the béarnaise mayonnaise on the side.

Grilled New York Strip Steaks SERVES 6

This method of cooking steaks on the grill is pure genius and I learned it from a master—Mark Lobel. Lobel's of New York is a fifth-generation butcher shop on Madison Avenue and it's one of the top butchers in the country. I season these steaks with a rub that Mark taught me but the real secret is in his grilling method. Perfect steak every time!

Kosher salt and freshly ground black pepper
2 teaspoons light brown sugar
2 teaspoons ground coffee (regular or decaf)
1 teaspoon (dried) granulated garlic
1 teaspoon chipotle chile powder
1 teaspoon crushed red pepper flakes
3 (1½-inch-thick) New York strip steaks
1½ tablespoons good olive oil

I use a charcoal chimney to heat the coals. With a gas grill, cook the steaks for 2 minutes on each side, then turn off 1 or 2 burners and place the steaks on the cool side of the grill to cook for 10 to 12 minutes.

In a small bowl, combine 2 tablespoons salt, 1 tablespoon black pepper, the brown sugar, coffee, garlic, chipotle powder, and red pepper flakes. Pat the steaks dry with paper towels, place them in a baking dish, and rub them all over with the olive oil. Rub the steaks on both sides with the spice mix, using it all. Cover the dish and refrigerate for at least 2 hours to allow the flavors to get into the meat.

When ready to cook, heat enough charcoal to cover half of the grill (I fill a charcoal chimney ¾ full). Pour a layer of hot coals on one side of the grill, leaving the other side empty.

Cook the steaks on the hot side of the grill for *exactly* 2 minutes on one side, turn them over, and cook for *exactly* 2 minutes on the other side. Move the steaks to the cool side of the grill, put the lid on, check to be sure the vents are open, and cook for 8 to 10 minutes, until an instant-read thermometer inserted sideways into the middle of the steak registers between 115 and 120 degrees for medium rare and 120 and 125 degrees for medium. Transfer the steaks to a plate, cover the plate tightly with aluminum foil, and allow to rest for 15 minutes. Remove the foil after 15 minutes or the steaks will continue to cook. Slice the steaks, sprinkle with salt, and serve hot or warm.

MAKE IT AHEAD: Coat the steaks with the spice rub, cover, and refrigerate for up to 1 day. Grill before dinner.

Rosemary Rack of Lamb with Easy Tzatziki serves 6

Rack of lamb is the easiest dinner I make for company. I slather the lamb with rosemary and garlic and let it sit in the fridge. All I need to do is roast the lamb for exactly 25 minutes and let it rest for 15, and it's ready to serve with the tzatziki.

1½ tablespoons chopped fresh rosemary leaves
1½ tablespoons chopped garlic (4 cloves)
1 tablespoon dried oregano
Kosher salt and freshly ground black pepper
2 tablespoons good olive oil
2 racks of lamb (14 to 16 ounces each), frenched
Easy Tzatziki (recipe follows)

Place the rosemary, garlic, oregano, 1 tablespoon salt, and 1½ teaspoons pepper in a food processor and process until minced. Add the olive oil and process into a coarse paste. Place the lamb on a sheet pan with the rib ends pointing down and spread the paste evenly on top of both racks. Cover and refrigerate for at least 6 hours.

When ready to cook, preheat the oven to 450 degrees.

Roast the lamb for 25 minutes exactly for medium rare and 30 minutes for medium. Remove from the oven and cover the pan tightly with aluminum foil. Allow the lamb to rest for 15 minutes. The internal temperature should read about 140 degrees when an instant-read thermometer is inserted sideways into the center of the lamb. Slice between the ribs into individual chops and serve hot or warm with Easy Tzatziki.

MAKE IT AHEAD: Rub the herb mixture on the lamb, wrap, and refrigerate it for up to 1 day. Roast the lamb before serving.

Easy Tzatziki MAKES 3 CUPS

Traditionally, tzatziki was made by draining salted cucumbers and yogurt overnight in the refrigerator to remove most of the liquid. Instead, I use Greek yogurt, which is already drained, and hothouse cucumbers, which have less liquid than traditional ones, so I can make this and serve it right away.

1 hothouse cucumber, unpeeled and seeded
2 (7-ounce) containers Greek yogurt, such as Fage Total
¼ cup sour cream
2 tablespoons freshly squeezed lemon juice
1 tablespoon white wine vinegar
1 tablespoon minced fresh dill
1½ teaspoons minced garlic (2 cloves)
Kosher salt and freshly ground black pepper

Grate the cucumber by hand on a box grater, as you would grate carrots. Squeeze the cucumber with your hands to remove a lot (but not all) of the liquid. Place in a medium bowl and stir in the yogurt, sour cream, lemon juice, vinegar, dill, garlic, 2 teaspoons salt, and ½ teaspoon pepper. Serve cold or at room temperature.

MAKE IT AHEAD: Prepare the tzatziki and refrigerate in a sealed container for up to a week.

Pastitsio <small>SERVES 8 TO 10</small>

Pastitsio is like a Greek lasagna. It takes a while to make but you can assemble it a day ahead and refrigerate it. The combination of beef, lamb, red wine, garlic, and cinnamon—plus the creamy, cheesy béchamel topping—makes this a really satisfying winter meal.

Good olive oil
1½ cups chopped yellow onion (1 large)
1 pound lean ground beef
1 pound lean ground lamb
½ cup dry red wine, such as Côtes du Rhône
1 tablespoon minced garlic (3 cloves)
1 tablespoon ground cinnamon
1 teaspoon dried oregano
1 teaspoon chopped fresh thyme leaves
Pinch of cayenne pepper
1 (28-ounce) can crushed tomatoes in thick purée,
  such as Red Pack
Kosher salt and freshly ground black pepper
1½ cups whole milk
1 cup heavy cream
4 tablespoons (½ stick) unsalted butter
¼ cup all-purpose flour
¼ teaspoon ground nutmeg
1½ cups freshly grated Parmesan cheese, divided
7 ounces Greek yogurt, such as Fage Total
12 ounces small pasta shells, such as Ronzoni
2 extra-large eggs, lightly beaten

Heat 3 tablespoons of olive oil in a large pot over medium to medium-high heat. Add the onion and sauté for 5 minutes. Add the beef and lamb and sauté over medium heat for 8 to 10 minutes, crumbling it with a wooden spoon, until it's no longer pink. Add the wine and cook for 2 minutes. Add the garlic, cinnamon, oregano, thyme, and cayenne, and continue cooking over medium heat for 5 minutes. Add the tomatoes and their liquid, 1 tablespoon salt, and 1½ teaspoons black pepper. Lower the heat and simmer, stirring occasionally, for 40 to 45 minutes, until the liquid evaporates. Set aside.

Preheat the oven to 350 degrees.

For the béchamel, heat the milk and cream together in a small saucepan over medium-low heat, until simmering. In a medium saucepan, melt the butter, add the flour, and cook over medium heat, whisking constantly, for 2 minutes. Pour the hot milk mixture into the butter and flour mixture, whisking constantly. Continue whisking over medium heat for 4 to 6 minutes, until thick and smooth. Add the nutmeg, 1 tablespoon salt, and 1 teaspoon black pepper. Stir in ¾ cup of the Parmesan cheese and allow to cool for 10 minutes. Stir in the yogurt and set aside.

Meanwhile, in a large pot of boiling salted water, cook the shells al dente, according to the package instructions. Don't overcook the pasta; it will be baked later. Drain and set aside.

To assemble, combine the pasta with the meat and tomato sauce, stir in the eggs, and pour the mixture into an 11 × 15 × 2-inch baking dish. Spread the béchamel evenly over the pasta and sprinkle with the remaining ¾ cup of Parmesan cheese. Bake for 1 hour, until golden brown and bubbly. Set aside for 10 minutes and serve hot.

MAKE IT AHEAD: Assemble the pastitsio completely and refrigerate for up to 2 days or freeze for up to 3 months. Defrost (if necessary) and bake before serving.

Roasted Vegetable Lasagna Serves 10

I've wrestled with all kinds of vegetable lasagnas. I love the flavor but the liquid in the vegetables always makes the lasagna watery. To solve the problem, I roasted the vegetables first and didn't precook the noodles, and the result is a delicious one-dish dinner. Herbed goat cheese, fresh ricotta, mozzarella, basil, and lots of Parmesan make it really satisfying.

1½ pounds eggplant, unpeeled, sliced lengthwise ¼ inch thick

¾ pound zucchini, unpeeled, sliced lengthwise ¼ inch thick

⅔ cup good olive oil

1 tablespoon dried oregano

Kosher salt and freshly ground black pepper

1 tablespoon minced garlic (3 cloves)

10 ounces lasagna noodles, such as De Cecco

16 ounces fresh whole-milk ricotta

8 ounces creamy garlic and herb goat cheese, at room temperature

2 extra-large eggs, lightly beaten

½ cup chopped fresh basil leaves, lightly packed

1 cup freshly grated Parmesan cheese, divided

4½ cups good bottled marinara sauce, such as Rao's (40 ounces)

1 pound lightly salted fresh mozzarella, very thinly sliced

Preheat the oven to 375 degrees. Arrange the eggplant and zucchini in single layers on 3 sheet pans lined with parchment paper. Brush them generously with the olive oil on both sides, using all of the oil. Sprinkle with the oregano (I crush it in my hands), 1 tablespoon salt, and 1½ teaspoons pepper. Roast for 25 minutes, sprinkle the garlic evenly on the vegetables, and roast for another 5 minutes, until the vegetables are cooked through. Remove from the oven and lower the temperature to 350 degrees.

Meanwhile, fill a very large bowl with the hottest tap water and add enough boiling water to bring the temperature to 140 degrees. One at a time, place the noodles in the water and

Make it ahead: Assemble the lasagna completely and refrigerate for up to 1 day or freeze for up to 3 months. Defrost (if necessary) and bake before dinner.

soak them for 15 minutes, swirling occasionally so they don't stick together. Drain and slide the noodles around again.

Combine the ricotta, goat cheese, eggs, basil, ½ cup of the Parmesan, 1½ teaspoons salt, and ¾ teaspoon pepper in the bowl of an electric mixer fitted with the paddle attachment and mix on low speed.

Spread 1 cup of the marinara in a 9 × 13 × 2-inch baking dish. Arrange a third of the vegetables on top, then a layer of the noodles (cut to fit), a third of the mozzarella, and a third of the ricotta mixture in large dollops between the mozzarella. Repeat twice, starting with the marinara. Spread the last 1½ cups of marinara on top and sprinkle with the remaining ½ cup of Parmesan. Place the dish on a sheet pan lined with parchment paper and bake for 60 to 70 minutes, until the lasagna is browned and bubbly. Allow to rest for 10 minutes and serve hot.

Herb-Roasted Fish serves 4

This is my new go-to dinner and without a doubt, it doesn't get any easier than this. It was inspired by a dish we were served at one of the great restaurants of the world—Ristorante Cibrèo in Florence. It's easy enough to make for a midweek dinner, but delicious enough to serve for company. The flavors of lemon, olives, and thyme really permeate the fish!

4 (12 × 16-inch) pieces of parchment paper

4 (8-ounce) boneless skin-on fish fillets, such as snapper or cod

Kosher salt and freshly ground black pepper

4 tablespoons good olive oil

4 tablespoons freshly squeezed lemon juice (2 lemons)

8 sprigs fresh thyme

8 Cerignola or other large green olives with pits

2 egg whites, lightly beaten

Preheat the oven to 400 degrees.

Place the pieces of parchment paper on a flat surface, fold them in half crosswise, and cut each piece like a large paper heart cutout. Open the fold flat and place each fillet lengthwise just to the right of the fold. On each fillet, sprinkle ½ teaspoon salt, ¼ teaspoon pepper, 1 tablespoon olive oil, 1 tablespoon lemon juice, and 2 sprigs of thyme, and place 2 olives alongside the fish.

Brush the edges of the entire parchment paper with the egg whites. Fold the left side of the parchment paper over the right side so the edges line up, creating a packet. Press the edges together to create a seal. Starting at the edge at the top of the heart, make overlapping folds in the parchment, until you reach the "tail" of the heart. Fold the last end underneath to seal the packet. Place all the packets on sheet pans, making sure the oil and lemon juice don't run out when you transfer them. Bake for 15 minutes exactly. Place each packet on a dinner plate, cut an X in the middle with scissors, and serve hot, allowing each person to tear open the packet.

See following page for wrapping instructions.

make it ahead: Prepare the packages and refrigerate for up to 1 day. Bake before serving.

Easy Coquilles Saint Jacques SERVES 6

This is one of the recipes I've been making for dinner parties since I was first married. I love the combination of sweet scallops, earthy mushrooms, Cognac, and Gruyère with crispy bread crumbs on top. Best of all, you can assemble it early and bake it right before dinner.

8 tablespoons (1 stick) unsalted butter, divided

¼ cup all-purpose flour

1½ cups seafood stock or clam juice

1 cup heavy cream

½ teaspoon curry powder

Kosher salt and freshly ground black pepper

1 cup small-diced shallots (4 large)

12 ounces cremini mushrooms, caps brushed clean, stems discarded

¼ cup Cognac or brandy

1½ cups fresh bread crumbs (see note)

¼ cup minced fresh flat-leaf parsley

5 ounces grated Gruyère cheese

¼ cup good olive oil

2 pounds fresh bay scallops, drained, side muscles removed (see note)

For fresh bread crumbs, remove the crusts from 6 slices of white sandwich bread, dice, and pulse in a food processor fitted with the steel blade, until it forms crumbs.

You can substitute 2 pounds of sea scallops, quartered, for the bay scallops.

Preheat the oven to 400 degrees and place six (1½-cup) gratin dishes on 2 sheet pans.

Melt 4 tablespoons of the butter over medium heat in a medium saucepan. Add the flour and cook for 2 minutes, whisking constantly. Add the seafood stock and whisk until it is smooth and thickened. Whisk in the cream, curry powder, 1½ teaspoons salt, and ½ teaspoon pepper. Bring the sauce to a boil, lower the heat, and simmer for 10 minutes, stirring occasionally. Set aside.

Heat the remaining 4 tablespoons of butter in a large (12-inch) sauté pan over medium-low heat. Add the shallots and sauté for 2 to 3 minutes, until tender. Slice the mushroom caps ½ inch thick, add to the shallots, and cook for 8 minutes, stirring often. Add the Cognac and cook for 1 to 2 minutes, until most of the

MAKE IT AHEAD: Assemble the gratins completely, cover, and refrigerate for up to a day. Bake before dinner.

liquid has evaporated. Sprinkle with 1 teaspoon salt and ½ teaspoon pepper and set aside.

Combine the bread crumbs, parsley, Gruyère, and olive oil in a medium bowl and stir to moisten the crumbs. Set aside.

Add the mushrooms to the cream sauce. Add the scallops and 1½ teaspoons salt, mix well, and divide among the gratin dishes. Sprinkle the bread crumb mixture evenly on top and bake for 20 minutes, until the scallops are cooked and the sauce is lightly browned and bubbly. Serve hot.

Provençal Fish Stew with Sriracha Rouille

SERVES 6

I love bouillabaisse but it takes a long time to prepare. This is a simplified version with all the Provençal flavor and none of the stress.

6 tablespoons good olive oil

1½ cups chopped yellow onion (1 large)

1½ cups (¾-inch-diced) Holland yellow bell pepper (1 large)

2½ cups (½-inch-diced) fennel bulb (1 large)

1 teaspoon saffron threads

Pinch of crushed red pepper flakes

4 oil-packed anchovies, drained and minced

¼ cup minced garlic (8 large cloves)

1 cup dry white wine

2 tablespoons Pernod

3 cups good seafood stock

1 (28-ounce) can diced tomatoes, such as San Marzano

1 (1 × 3-inch) strip of orange zest

¾ cup freshly squeezed orange juice (3 oranges)

Kosher salt and freshly ground black pepper

1½ pounds fresh cod fillets, skinned and cut in 2-inch dice

1½ pounds fresh halibut or monkfish fillets, skinned and cut in 2-inch dice

36 fresh mussels, scrubbed and debearded

¼ cup minced fresh flat-leaf parsley

12 large diagonal slices of French bread, toasted

Sriracha Rouille (recipe follows)

In a large pot or Dutch oven, such as Le Creuset, heat the olive oil over medium heat. Add the onion, bell pepper, fennel, saffron, and red pepper flakes and cook for 15 minutes, stirring occasionally, until the vegetables are tender. Add the anchovies and garlic and cook for one minute, stirring occasionally. Add the wine and Pernod, bring to a boil, and cook for 2 minutes.

MAKE IT AHEAD: Prepare the soup stock, cool to room temperature, and refrigerate for up to 24 hours. When ready to serve, reheat the stock, stir in the fish and mussels, and finish the recipe.

Add the seafood stock, tomatoes, orange zest, orange juice, 1 tablespoon salt, and 1½ teaspoons black pepper. Bring to a boil, lower the heat, and simmer uncovered for 25 minutes, stirring occasionally. Discard the orange zest and stir in the cod and halibut. Raise the heat and simmer uncovered for 5 minutes, until the fish *just* begins to flake. (Don't stir from now on, or you will break up the fish!) Place the mussels on top, cover, and simmer for 5 minutes, until the mussels just open. (Discard any that don't open.) Gently fold in the parsley and serve hot in large shallow bowls with 2 slices of toasted French bread spread generously with the Sriracha Rouille.

Sriracha Rouille MAKES ¾ CUP

Rouille is a garlicky mayonnaise that's traditionally served on toast or spooned into bouillabaisse. I updated it with Sriracha, a Thai hot pepper sauce, and it's wonderful with the Provençal Fish Stew.

1 tablespoon minced garlic (3 cloves)
1 teaspoon kosher salt
½ teaspoon saffron threads
1 extra-large egg yolk, at room temperature
1½ tablespoons freshly squeezed lemon juice, at room temperature
1 teaspoon Sriracha
1 cup good olive oil, at room temperature

Place the garlic, salt, and saffron in a food processor fitted with the steel blade and purée. Add the egg yolk, lemon juice, and Sriracha, and process for 5 to 7 seconds.

With the machine running, gradually pour the olive oil through the feed tube in a thin, steady stream to make a thick emulsion like mayonnaise.

MAKE IT AHEAD: Prepare and refrigerate in a sealed container for up to a week.

Garlic & Herb Roasted Shrimp serves 4

A few years ago, I started roasting shrimp for shrimp cocktail instead of boiling them. It was so successful—and so easy!—that I decided to use the same technique for a main-course dish. These shrimp are flavored with butter, garlic, rosemary, and lots of lemon and I bring the pan right from the oven to the table.

I serve this with basmati rice and steamed broccoli, which are great with the garlicky butter sauce.

¼ pound (1 stick) unsalted butter
2 tablespoons good olive oil
2 tablespoons minced garlic (6 cloves)
2 teaspoons minced fresh rosemary leaves
¼ teaspoon crushed red pepper flakes
Kosher salt and freshly ground black pepper
2 large lemons
2 pounds (8- to 10-count) shrimp, peeled with the tails on
1 teaspoon coarse sea salt
4 slices country bread, toasted

Preheat the oven to 400 degrees.

Melt the butter over low heat in a medium (10-inch) sauté pan. Add the olive oil, garlic, rosemary, red pepper flakes, 1 teaspoon kosher salt, and ½ teaspoon black pepper and cook over low heat for one minute. Off the heat, zest one of the lemons directly into the butter mixture.

Meanwhile, arrange the shrimp snugly in one layer in a large (12-inch) round ovenproof sauté pan (or 10 × 13-inch baking dish) with only the tails overlapping. Pour the butter mixture over the shrimp. Sprinkle with the sea salt and ½ teaspoon black pepper. Slice the ends off the zested lemon, cut five (¼-inch-thick) slices, and tuck them among the shrimp. Roast for 12 to 15 minutes, just until the shrimp are firm, pink, and cooked through. Cut the remaining lemon in half and squeeze the juice onto the shrimp. Serve hot with the toasted bread for dipping into the garlic butter.

MAKE IT AHEAD: Prep the dish and refrigerate it in the pan. Roast before serving.

vegetables

Asparagus & Prosciutto Bundles

Spinach & Ricotta Noodle Pudding

Roasted Baby Bok Choy

Crusty Baked Potatoes with Whipped Feta

Make-Ahead Goat Cheese Mashed Potatoes

Peas & Pancetta

Pear & Parsnip Gratin

Braised Red Cabbage with Pancetta

Gingered Basmati Rice

Summer Vegetable Couscous

Carrot & Cauliflower Purée

Roasted Cauliflower Snowflakes

Baked Farro & Butternut Squash

Baked Polenta with
Mushrooms & Blue Cheese

Stuffed Zucchini

Parmesan Chive Smashed Potatoes

Leek & Artichoke Bread Pudding

Twice-Baked Sweet Potatoes

10 tips for safely storing food

1. Check sell-by dates on all fresh food, such as milk and yogurt, to be sure you use them before they spoil.

2. Put proteins, such as meat and fish, on the bottom shelves of the fridge so they don't accidentally drip onto things like fruit or cheese that you might be eating without cooking. Place a plate or tray under the packages to catch drips.

3. Most meat, except ground meat, lasts for 3 or 4 days in the refrigerator. Ground meats should be used within a day or two.

4. Cool cooked food almost to room temperature before refrigerating or freezing. Storing hot food will raise the temperature of the refrigerator and compromise the other food.

5. Test your refrigerator with a thermometer to be sure it stays between 38 and 42 degrees and the freezer stays below 0 degrees.

6. Plastic wrap stretches best on the diagonal when you're wrapping dishes or food. I use Stretch-Tite plastic wrap, which is available in grocery stores and at Amazon.com.

7. Wrap dishes of food both over *and* under the dish to create a tight seal.

8. Air is the enemy of food stored in the refrigerator or freezer. Push excess air out of plastic storage bags and store refrigerated food in properly sized bowls or containers.

9. Don't stack containers or dishes in the fridge so the food cools quickly.

10. Most cooked food can be stored in the refrigerator for about a week, except fish, which should only be stored for a day or two.

Asparagus & Prosciutto Bundles SERVES 6

Asparagus is one of my favorite vegetables and this is how I serve it for a special dinner. Truffle butter, crispy prosciutto, and Gruyère cheese make these roasted asparagus really delicious.

Kosher salt
2 pounds medium-size asparagus, bottom
   thirds discarded
6 slices of Italian prosciutto
Good olive oil
2 tablespoons white truffle butter
Fleur de sel and freshly ground black pepper
2 ounces grated Gruyère cheese

Preheat the oven to 400 degrees.

Fill a large pot with water, add 1 tablespoon salt, and bring to a boil. If the asparagus are thick, peel them halfway up the stalk with a vegetable peeler. Immerse the asparagus in the boiling water and cook for 2 minutes. Drain the asparagus and put them immediately into a large bowl of ice water to set the bright green color. Allow to chill for 2 to 3 minutes. Drain and pat the asparagus dry.

Gather 6 to 8 asparagus spears into a bundle with the tips together, and wrap a slice of prosciutto securely around the middle. Repeat to make 6 bundles. Brush a rectangular baking dish (large enough to hold the bundles in one layer) with 1½ tablespoons of olive oil. Place the bundles seam side down in the baking dish, arranged side by side, with the tips facing the same way. In a small saucepan, heat the truffle butter and 1½ tablespoons of olive oil until the butter melts. Drizzle it over the bundles. Sprinkle with ¾ teaspoon fleur de sel, ½ teaspoon pepper, and the Gruyère and bake for 12 to 15 minutes, until the butter is sizzling and the cheese melts and starts to brown. Serve hot.

MAKE IT AHEAD: Assemble the asparagus bundles, top with truffle butter and cheese, and refrigerate for up to 12 hours. Bake before serving.

Spinach & Ricotta Noodle Pudding

SERVES 12

For the Jewish holidays, I often make a traditional noodle kugel. This year, I added spinach, ricotta, fresh dill, and a nice crunchy panko crust. It's a little like a mash-up of noodle kugel and spanakopita, and it was so good!

Kosher salt and freshly ground black pepper

12 ounces wide egg noodles, such as David's

4 tablespoons good olive oil, divided

2 cups chopped yellow onions (2 onions)

¾ cup sliced scallions, white and green parts (4 scallions)

1 cup fresh whole-milk ricotta

4 cups half-and-half

5 extra-large eggs

¼ cup minced fresh dill

1 cup plus 2 tablespoons freshly grated Parmesan cheese, divided

1 (9-ounce) package frozen chopped spinach, defrosted

1 cup panko (Japanese bread flakes)

Preheat the oven to 350 degrees. Butter a 13 × 10 × 2-inch oval baking dish.

Cook the noodles in a large pot of boiling salted water, according to the directions on the package. Drain and set aside.

In a medium (10-inch) sauté pan, heat 2 tablespoons of the olive oil, add the onions, and sauté over medium-low heat for 15 minutes, stirring occasionally, until tender but not browned. Add the scallions and cook for 2 minutes. Set aside.

Meanwhile, combine the ricotta, half-and-half, eggs, dill, 1 cup of the Parmesan, 4 teaspoons salt, and 1 teaspoon pepper in a bowl. Squeeze most, but not all, of the water out of the spinach and mix it into the ricotta mixture. Mix in the onion mixture and noodles and pour into the prepared dish.

In a small bowl, combine the panko, the remaining 2 tablespoons of olive oil, and the remaining 2 tablespoons of Parmesan. Sprinkle the mixture on the pudding. Place the dish in a roasting pan large enough to hold the baking dish and pour hot tap water

MAKE IT AHEAD: Assemble the pudding, cover, and refrigerate for up to a day. Bake before serving.

halfway up the side of the dish. Bake for 45 minutes, remove the dish from the water bath, and bake for 15 to 20 minutes, until the top is golden brown and a knife inserted in the middle comes out clean. Allow to cool for 5 minutes and serve hot.

Roasted Baby Bok Choy serves 6

Bok choy used to be available only in Asian markets but now you can find it in your local grocery store. Look for small baby bok choy if you can find them. Toss them with olive oil, salt, and pepper and pop them into the oven. It's the most surprisingly delicious vegetable and takes only minutes to prepare.

12 small baby bok choy (similar sizes)
Good olive oil
Kosher salt and freshly ground black pepper

Preheat the oven to 375 degrees.

Remove any wilted leaves from the bok choy, then cut off the top half of the largest leaves and discard. Wash the bok choy and shake off any excess water. Cut each head of bok choy in half through the core, leaving the cores intact. Place on two sheet pans, drizzle with olive oil, sprinkle with salt and pepper, and toss. Turn the bok choy cut sides down and roast for 20 minutes, until the small core is just tender. Sprinkle with salt and serve hot.

MAKE IT AHEAD: Prep the bok choy and store in a plastic storage bag with a slightly damp paper towel for up to 3 days. Season and roast before serving.

Crusty Baked Potatoes with Whipped Feta serves 4

Jeffrey loves baked potatoes and I'm always looking for ways to make them special. I bake these with a crust of rosemary, thyme, and lemon zest and then serve a big bowl of whipped feta with lemon and chives to dollop on top.

1 tablespoon chopped fresh rosemary
2 teaspoons fresh thyme leaves
Grated zest of 1 large lemon
1 tablespoon coarse fleur de sel or sea salt
4 large (8- to 10-ounce) Idaho baking potatoes
Good olive oil
Whipped Feta (recipe follows)
Chopped fresh chives

Preheat the oven to 400 degrees. Line a sheet pan with aluminum foil.

Place the rosemary, thyme, lemon zest, and fleur de sel in the bowl of a mini food processor and pulse 10 to 12 times, until finely chopped but not puréed. Spread the mixture in a shallow bowl or plate.

Scrub the potatoes, dry them well, and pierce them all over with the tines of a fork. Place the potatoes on the prepared sheet pan and rub them all over with olive oil. Roll each potato in the salt and herb mixture and put them back on the sheet pan. Bake for 60 to 75 minutes, until tender. Slit the top of each potato, squeeze the ends together to open the potato, and top with a generous scoop of whipped feta. Sprinkle with chives and serve hot with extra whipped feta on the side.

MAKE IT AHEAD: Prepare the whipped feta and the lemon and herb mixture, and refrigerate separately for up to 5 days. Before dinner, rub the potatoes with oil, roll them in the herb mixture, and bake.

Whipped Feta SERVES 4

6 ounces Greek feta, crumbled
2 ounces cream cheese, at room temperature
⅓ cup good olive oil
2 tablespoons freshly squeezed lemon juice
Kosher salt and freshly ground black pepper

Place the feta and cream cheese in the bowl of a food processor fitted with the steel blade and pulse until the cheeses are mixed. Add the olive oil, lemon juice, ½ teaspoon salt, and ¼ teaspoon pepper and process until smooth. Refrigerate until ready to serve.

Make-Ahead Goat Cheese Mashed Potatoes SERVES 6 TO 8

It is a myth that mashed potatoes need to be made just before they're served. They can go into a heat-proof bowl set over simmering water for about thirty minutes, as long as you keep adding more liquid to keep them creamy. Or, even easier, I pour them into a baking dish, sprinkle with Parmesan cheese, and bake them in the oven.

3 pounds large Yukon Gold potatoes, peeled and cut in
    ¾-inch chunks
5 large garlic cloves
Kosher salt and freshly ground black pepper
7 to 8 ounces garlic and herb goat cheese, at room
    temperature, such as Montrachet
4 tablespoons (½ stick) unsalted butter, at room temperature
1½ cups sour cream
½ cup half-and-half or milk
½ cup freshly grated Parmesan cheese

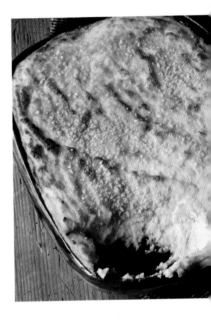

Preheat the oven to 375 degrees.

Place the potatoes, garlic, and 1 tablespoon of salt in a large pot with enough water to cover the potatoes. Bring to a boil over high heat, reduce to a simmer, and cook for 20 to 25 minutes, until very tender.

Drain the potatoes and garlic and process them together through a food mill fitted with the coarsest blade set over a bowl. While the potatoes are still hot, stir in the goat cheese, butter, sour cream, half-and-half, 4 teaspoons salt, and 2 teaspoons pepper, until smooth.

Pour the mixture into a 9 × 12 × 2-inch oval baking dish, smoothing the top. Sprinkle the Parmesan on top and bake for 30 to 40 minutes, until lightly browned. Serve hot.

MAKE IT AHEAD: Assemble the dish, including the Parmesan, and refrigerate for up to 3 days. Bake before serving.

Peas & Pancetta serves 4 to 5

Peas and pancetta is a classic old-world Italian side dish but too often the peas are totally overcooked. I decided to try sautéing the pancetta first and then adding the peas for the last 4 or 5 minutes of cooking so they stayed nice and green. Some fresh mint from the garden added the perfect note.

Ask the store to slice the pancetta ¼ inch thick so you can cut it in ¼-inch dice.

1 tablespoon good olive oil
2½ ounces pancetta, ¼-inch-diced (see note)
1 large shallot, halved and sliced
1 (10-ounce) box frozen peas, such as Birds Eye Garden Peas
Kosher salt and freshly ground black pepper
1 tablespoon julienned fresh mint leaves

Heat the olive oil in a medium (10-inch) sauté pan, add the pancetta and shallot, and cook over medium heat for 5 to 7 minutes, stirring occasionally, until the pancetta is browned and the shallot is tender. Add the frozen peas, 1 teaspoon salt, and ¼ teaspoon pepper and cook over medium-low heat for 4 to 5 minutes, until the peas are hot. Stir in the mint, taste for seasonings, and serve hot.

MAKE IT AHEAD: Sauté the pancetta and shallots and set aside. Before serving, reheat, add the peas, and finish the recipe.

Pear & Parsnip Gratin SERVES 6 TO 8

*Purées are great to make in advance because they reheat so well. I put
the pear and parsnip purée in a baking dish with some eggs, sour cream,
orange zest, and ginger and bake it before dinner.*

1¾ pounds parsnips, unpeeled, trimmed and cut in
    1-inch chunks
3 Bosc pears, unpeeled, cored and cut in 1-inch chunks
3 tablespoons unsalted butter, small-diced
½ cup sour cream
2 extra-large eggs, lightly beaten
¾ teaspoon grated orange zest
¾ teaspoon ground ginger
Kosher salt and freshly ground black pepper

*Parsnips are a great winter
vegetable.*

Preheat the oven to 350 degrees.

Place the parsnips, pears, and 2 cups of water in a large
saucepan and bring to a boil. Lower the heat, cover, and cook
for 15 to 20 minutes, until the parsnips and pears are both very
tender. With a slotted spoon, transfer them into a food mill fitted
with the coarsest blade set over a bowl, and process.

Meanwhile, combine the butter, sour cream, eggs, orange zest,
ginger, 2½ teaspoons salt, and 1 teaspoon pepper in a medium
bowl. Whisk in the hot purée, pour it into a 9 × 12 × 1½-inch oval
gratin dish, and smooth the top. Bake for 40 to 45 minutes, until
slightly puffed and golden on top. Serve hot.

MAKE IT AHEAD: Assemble
the gratin, cover, and refrigerate for up to 3 days. Bake before
serving.

Braised Red Cabbage with Pancetta

SERVES 6

On a cold winter night, braised cabbage can be a very satisfying side dish for pork, poultry, or game. This version is simmered with good red wine, apples, and a splash of balsamic vinegar to wake it up. This can be made days in advance and reheated on top of the stove.

1 tablespoon good olive oil

½ pound pancetta, ½-inch-diced

4 cups yellow onions, halved lengthwise and sliced ½ inch thick (3 onions)

1 cup good red wine, such as Burgundy

⅓ cup apple cider vinegar

1 (2-pound) red cabbage, grated (see note)

3 firm red apples, such as Macoun, unpeeled, halved, cored, and sliced ¼ inch thick

¼ cup light brown sugar, lightly packed

Kosher salt and freshly ground black pepper

1 tablespoon balsamic vinegar

Grate the cabbage in a food processor fitted with the slicing disk. Cut the cabbage in quarters, remove the cores, cut in wedges to fit sideways in the feed tube (for longer shreds), and process.

Heat the olive oil in a large pot or Dutch oven, such as Le Creuset, add the pancetta, and sauté over medium heat for 6 to 8 minutes, until browned. Remove the pancetta with a slotted spoon to a plate lined with paper towels and set aside. Add the onions and cook for another 8 to 10 minutes, until the onions are lightly browned. Add the red wine and cider vinegar and scrape up the brown bits in the pan. Add the cabbage, apples, brown sugar, 4 teaspoons salt, and 2 teaspoons pepper. Bring to a boil, cover, then lower the heat and simmer for 1 hour, checking occasionally to be sure there is still liquid in the pan. (Add a little water if it's dry.) Remove the lid and cook, stirring occasionally, over medium-low heat for another 30 to 45 minutes, until most of the liquid evaporates. Stir in the reserved pancetta and the balsamic vinegar, taste for seasonings, and serve hot.

MAKE IT AHEAD: Prepare completely and refrigerate for up to 4 days. Reheat slowly on top of the stove, adding more water or wine, if necessary.

Gingered Basmati Rice serves 4 to 6

My friend Barbara Liberman introduced me to her favorite rice dish and wow—this is no ordinary rice! Fresh ginger, sautéed onions, thyme, and scallions make this a great side for chicken, pork, and shrimp.

2 tablespoons good olive oil
½ cup chopped yellow onion
1 tablespoon minced fresh ginger
2¾ cups good chicken stock, preferably homemade (page 62)
½ teaspoon chopped fresh thyme leaves
½ cup chopped scallions, white and green parts (3 scallions)
1½ cups brown basmati rice, such as Texmati
Kosher salt and freshly ground black pepper

Heat the olive oil in a medium heavy-bottomed saucepan over medium-low heat, add the onion and ginger, and cook for 5 minutes. Add the chicken stock, thyme, scallions, rice, 1 teaspoon salt, and ½ teaspoon pepper and bring to a boil. Lower the heat, cover, and simmer for 45 minutes, until the rice is tender. Stir occasionally while cooking to be sure the rice doesn't stick to the bottom of the pot. Serve hot.

MAKE IT AHEAD: Prepare the rice completely and refrigerate. Add a little water, cover, and reheat over low heat on top of the stove.

Summer Vegetable Couscous serves 6 to 8

This is another recipe inspired by Sarah Leah Chase, who writes
wonderful cookbooks. It has many Middle Eastern flavors and textures
that all complement each other: couscous with cinnamon and ginger plus
raisins, dates, chickpeas, and toasted almonds. In summer, it's the perfect
accompaniment to grilled chicken or fish.

3 cups good chicken stock, preferably homemade (page 62)
Good olive oil
1½ teaspoons ground turmeric
1½ teaspoons ground cinnamon
1½ teaspoons ground ginger
Kosher salt and freshly ground black pepper
2 cups couscous
¼ cup golden raisins
¼ cup diced dried pitted dates
1 medium zucchini, ¼-inch-diced
2 carrots, ¼-inch-diced
½ red onion, ¼-inch-diced
½ cup canned chickpeas, rinsed and drained
¼ cup freshly squeezed lemon juice (2 lemons)
½ cup blanched sliced almonds, toasted (see note)

Place the chicken stock, 2 tablespoons olive oil, the turmeric,
cinnamon, ginger, 1 teaspoon salt, and ½ teaspoon pepper in a
large saucepan and bring to a boil. Off the heat, stir in the couscous, raisins, and dates; cover, and set aside for 15 minutes.

In a large bowl, combine the zucchini, carrots, red onion,
and chickpeas. Fluff the couscous with a fork and add it to the
vegetables.

Whisk together the lemon juice and ¼ cup of olive oil and
pour it over the couscous. Carefully fold in the toasted almonds,
taste for seasonings, and serve at room temperature. The flavors
will meld the longer it sits.

To toast almonds, place them
in a small sauté pan over low
heat and cook for 5 to 7 minutes,
tossing frequently, until lightly
browned.

MAKE IT AHEAD: Prepare the
couscous completely, cover,
and refrigerate for up to 2 days.
Serve at room temperature.

Carrot & Cauliflower Purée serves 5 to 6

At one of my favorite restaurants in Paris, I was served a simple carrot purée that had an elusive flavor, so I asked the waiter for the secret. He whispered that it was browned butter—what the French call beurre noisette. *It was such a simple ingredient that completely transformed this vegetable purée.*

Kosher salt and freshly ground black pepper
1 medium head cauliflower, core removed, and cut into
     florets
1½ pounds carrots, unpeeled and cut into 1-inch chunks
     (see note)
4 ounces good salted butter, such as Président

I prefer "topped" carrots that are sold with the greens attached because they're fresher and sweeter.

Bring a large pot of water to a boil. Add 2 tablespoons of salt and the cauliflower and boil for 20 minutes, until the cauliflower is very tender. Remove the cauliflower to a bowl, using a slotted spoon or strainer. Add the carrots to the boiling water and cook for another 20 minutes, until very tender. Drain the carrots and add them to the cauliflower. (Do them separately, light-colored vegetables first, since they might not cook in the same amount of time.) Place a food mill fitted with the medium disk over a large saucepan and process the vegetables into the pan.

Meanwhile, melt the butter in a small (8-inch) sauté pan over medium-low heat and cook until the milk solids in the pan turn golden brown. Watch the butter carefully because it will turn black very quickly! Whisk the browned butter plus 2 teaspoons of salt and 1 teaspoon of pepper into the vegetable purée. Taste for seasonings, reheat over low heat, and serve hot.

MAKE IT AHEAD: Prepare completely and refrigerate for up to 4 days. Reheat over low heat on top of the stove.

Roasted Cauliflower Snowflakes SERVES 4

Irene Danilovitch prepared this roasted cauliflower for a friend, who made it for me. I love the way it looks, it's beyond easy to prepare, and it's surprisingly delicious. Now I serve cauliflower this way all the time!

I grate the Parmesan on a box grater, as you would grate carrots.

1 head cauliflower (about 2½ pounds)
Good olive oil
Kosher salt and freshly ground black pepper
½ cup panko (Japanese bread flakes)
½ cup freshly grated Parmesan cheese (see note)

Preheat the oven to 425 degrees.

Remove the leaves and trim the stem of the cauliflower but leave the core intact. With a sharp slicing knife, cut the whole cauliflower in large (½-inch-thick) slices. Don't worry if the slices fall apart; they'll look like snowflakes. Place the cauliflower on a sheet pan, drizzle with 3 tablespoons of olive oil, and sprinkle with ¾ teaspoon salt and ¼ teaspoon pepper. Roast the cauliflower for 15 minutes.

Toss the panko with 1 tablespoon of olive oil, sprinkle on the cauliflower, and roast for another 10 to 15 minutes, until tender and browned. Sprinkle with the Parmesan and roast for another minute or two. Immediately, scrape the pan with a metal spatula and toss the cauliflower and Parmesan. Serve hot or at room temperature.

MAKE IT AHEAD: Cut the cauliflower, place it in a plastic storage bag with a damp paper towel, and refrigerate for up to 3 days. Roast and complete the recipe before dinner.

Baked Farro & Butternut Squash

SERVES 6 TO 8

This is a recipe from California chef Maria Sinskey. It's delicious as a side dish with a roast chicken but it's hearty enough to be served as a main course. The flavors and textures of the sweet butternut squash, earthy farro, smoky applewood bacon, and good chicken stock are amazing.

6 thick-cut slices applewood-smoked bacon
2 tablespoons good olive oil
1 tablespoon unsalted butter
1½ cups chopped yellow onion (1 large)
2 teaspoons chopped fresh thyme leaves
Kosher salt and freshly ground black pepper
1½ cups pearled farro
3 cups good chicken stock, preferably homemade
    (page 62)
3 cups (¾- to 1-inch-diced) butternut squash
½ cup freshly grated Parmesan cheese

Peel butternut squash and cut it in half so it doesn't wobble while you dice it.

Preheat the oven to 375 degrees.

Place the bacon on a baking rack set on a sheet pan and bake it for 20 to 30 minutes, until browned (it won't be crisp). Cut the bacon in very large dice.

Meanwhile, in a small (9-inch) Dutch oven, such as Le Creuset, heat the olive oil and butter over medium heat. Add the onion and cook for 6 to 8 minutes, until tender and starting to brown. Add the thyme, 2 teaspoons salt, and 1 teaspoon pepper and cook for one minute. Add the farro and chicken stock and bring to a simmer. Place the squash on top of the farro mixture, cover, and bake in the same oven with the bacon for 30 minutes, until the squash and farro are tender. Check once during cooking and add a little chicken stock if it's dry.

Sprinkle the bacon and Parmesan on the squash and farro and bake uncovered for 15 to 20 minutes, until most of the liquid evaporates, the farro and butternut squash are tender, and the cheese has melted. Serve hot directly from the pot.

MAKE IT AHEAD: Assemble the dish, including the bacon and Parmesan, and refrigerate for up to 2 days. Bake before serving.

Baked Polenta with Mushrooms & Blue Cheese SERVES 6

This is another side dish that's also hearty enough for a main course. To make it vegetarian, substitute good vegetable stock. What could be more comforting than creamy polenta with meaty roasted portobello mushrooms topped with melted sharp blue cheese?

6 large portobello mushrooms (about 1½ pounds), stems discarded
3 tablespoons good olive oil
1 tablespoon balsamic vinegar
Kosher salt and freshly ground black pepper
2½ cups good chicken stock, preferably homemade (page 62)
2 cups half-and-half
¾ cup fine cornmeal
¼ cup imported Italian mascarpone cheese
4 ounces Gorgonzola piccante, crumbled

Preheat the oven to 400 degrees.

Brush the mushroom caps gently with a clean cloth to wipe away any dirt. Arrange them, underside up, on a sheet pan, drizzle with the olive oil and balsamic vinegar, then sprinkle with 1 teaspoon salt and ½ teaspoon pepper. Bake for 20 minutes, until tender. Set aside. Lower the oven to 375 degrees.

Meanwhile, make the polenta. Pour the stock and half-and-half into a large saucepan and bring it to a boil. Lower the heat and, while whisking constantly, slowly sprinkle the cornmeal into the boiling liquid. Simmer for 6 to 8 minutes, stirring almost constantly with a wooden spoon, until the polenta is thick and smooth. Off the heat, stir in the mascarpone, 1 teaspoon salt, and ½ teaspoon pepper. Pour into an 8 × 11 × 2-inch baking dish.

Arrange the mushrooms, underside up, in one layer over the polenta. Sprinkle on the Gorgonzola and bake for 25 to 30 minutes, until the polenta is bubbly and the cheese is melted. Sprinkle with salt and serve hot.

MAKE IT AHEAD: Roast the mushrooms and make the polenta. Assemble the dish and allow to sit at room temperature for up to 2 hours. Bake before serving.

Stuffed Zucchini SERVES 5 TO 6

Zucchini lend themselves beautifully to being stuffed. I cut them in half lengthwise, scoop out the seeds, and then fill the cavities with sourdough croutons, tomatoes, scallions, garlic, and thyme. Choose similarly sized zucchini so they all cook in the same amount of time.

5 to 6 small zucchini, trimmed (1½ pounds total)
Good olive oil
1 cup (½-inch-diced) sourdough bread, crusts removed
¼ cup sliced scallions, white and green parts (2 scallions)
1½ cups (½-inch-diced) tomatoes (2 tomatoes)
2 teaspoons minced fresh thyme leaves
2 teaspoons minced garlic (2 cloves)
2 tablespoons freshly grated Parmesan cheese
Kosher salt and freshly ground black pepper
1½ cups grated Gruyère cheese (4 ounces)

Preheat the oven to 450 degrees.

Fill a large pot with water and bring to a boil. Add the zucchini and simmer for 8 to 10 minutes, until tender. Remove to a plate lined with paper towels. When cool enough to handle, cut the zucchini in half lengthwise, scoop out the seeds with a small spoon, and place, cut side down, on the paper towels.

Meanwhile, heat 2 tablespoons of olive oil in a small (8-inch) sauté pan, add the bread cubes, and cook over medium-low heat for 5 minutes, tossing frequently until golden brown. Transfer to a medium bowl. In the same pan, heat 1 tablespoon of olive oil, add the scallions, tomatoes, thyme, and garlic, and cook over medium heat for 5 minutes, tossing frequently. Add to the bowl with the bread cubes. Add the Parmesan, 1½ teaspoons salt, and ½ teaspoon pepper and toss gently.

Place the zucchini snugly in a 10 × 14-inch rectangular baking dish in one layer, cut sides up. Sprinkle with 1½ teaspoons salt and ½ teaspoon pepper. With a small spoon, fill the cavities with the tomato and bread mixture. Sprinkle with the Gruyère and bake for 10 to 12 minutes, until lightly browned. Serve hot.

MAKE IT AHEAD: Assemble the stuffed zucchini, wrap, and refrigerate for up to 6 hours. Bake before serving.

Parmesan Chive Smashed Potatoes

SERVES 4 TO 6

This is a great way to cook potatoes! Boil them first, then smash them on a sheet pan, and finally roast them at a high temperature. You end up with tender creamy insides and lots of crispy edges. Grated Parmesan and fresh chives on top make them even better.

1 pound mixed small Yukon Gold and red new potatoes, scrubbed
Kosher salt and freshly ground black pepper
3 tablespoons good olive oil
½ cup freshly grated Parmesan cheese
2 tablespoons minced fresh chives
Fleur de sel or sea salt

Preheat the oven to 400 degrees.

Place the potatoes and 1 tablespoon salt in a large saucepan and add enough water to cover the potatoes. Bring to a boil, reduce the heat, and simmer for 17 to 20 minutes, until the potatoes are tender when pierced with a skewer. Drain the potatoes and place on a sheet pan. With a potato masher or metal measuring cup, press each potato until it's about ½ inch thick (they will be messy). Toss the potatoes with the olive oil, 1 teaspoon salt, and ¾ teaspoon pepper.

Roast the potatoes for 25 to 30 minutes, turning once, until the skins have become nicely browned. Sprinkle the potatoes with the Parmesan cheese and roast for another 2 to 3 minutes, just until the cheese melts. Sprinkle the potatoes with the chives and fleur de sel and serve hot.

MAKE IT AHEAD: Boil the potatoes and smash them on the sheet pan. Roast the potatoes and finish the recipe before serving.

Leek & Artichoke Bread Pudding serves 8

Instead of stuffing, I make a savory bread pudding that is moist inside and crispy on top. If you try this, you'll never go back to stuffing a turkey again!

8 cups (1-inch-diced) day-old bakery white bread, crusts removed
3 ounces thinly sliced pancetta
6 cups (½-inch-diced) leeks, white and light green parts (5 leeks)
3 tablespoons unsalted butter
½ cup dry white wine, such as Pinot Grigio
Kosher salt and freshly ground black pepper
1 (9-ounce) package frozen artichoke hearts, defrosted
3 tablespoons minced fresh chives
2 teaspoons minced fresh tarragon leaves
4 extra-large eggs
2 cups heavy cream
1 cup good chicken stock, preferably homemade (page 62)
¼ teaspoon ground nutmeg
2 cups grated Emmentaler Swiss cheese (8 ounces)

Frozen artichokes make this dish easier!

Preheat the oven to 350 degrees.

Place the bread cubes on a sheet pan and bake for 15 minutes, tossing once, until lightly browned. Place the pancetta in one layer on another sheet pan and bake in the same oven for 15 to 20 minutes, until lightly browned. Place the pancetta on a plate lined with paper towels and set aside.

Meanwhile, soak the leeks in water until they're clean, and spin them dry in a salad spinner. Heat the butter in an 11-inch pot over medium heat, add the leeks, and cook for 10 minutes, stirring occasionally. Add the wine, 1 teaspoon salt, and 1 teaspoon pepper and cook for 5 minutes, until the wine almost evaporates and the leeks are tender. Off the heat, mix in the artichokes, toasted bread cubes, chives, and tarragon.

Whisk the eggs, cream, chicken stock, nutmeg, and 1 teaspoon salt together in a large bowl. Spoon half of the bread mixture into a 13 × 9 × 2-inch baking dish. Sprinkle with half

MAKE IT AHEAD: Assemble the bread pudding and refrigerate for up to 2 days. Bake before serving.

the Emmentaler and add the remaining bread mixture. Pour on the cream mixture, sprinkle with the remaining Emmentaler, and press lightly to help the bread absorb the liquid. Dice or crumble the pancetta, scatter on top, and sprinkle lightly with pepper. Set aside at room temperature for 30 minutes to allow the bread to absorb the cream mixture. Bake for 45 to 50 minutes, until the custard is set and the bread pudding is puffed and golden. Serve hot.

Twice-Baked Sweet Potatoes SERVES 6

This is the perfect side dish for any roasted meat or poultry dinner. Bake the potatoes, scoop out half of the potato, mash with shallots, thyme, butter, and Taleggio cheese, and then pile it back into the potato shells. Try them at your next Thanksgiving!

3 medium sweet potatoes, scrubbed (12 to 14 ounces each)
5½ tablespoons unsalted butter, at room temperature, divided
½ cup minced shallots (2 shallots)
1 teaspoon minced fresh thyme leaves, plus 6 sprigs for garnish
Kosher salt and freshly ground black pepper
1 extra-large egg, lightly beaten
4 ounces Taleggio cheese, small-diced (6 ounces with the rind)

Preheat the oven to 400 degrees. Line a sheet pan with aluminum foil.

Place the potatoes on the prepared sheet pan and cut a few slits in each potato to allow steam to escape. Bake the potatoes for 50 minutes to 1 hour, until very tender when tested with a skewer. Set aside for 10 minutes, until cool enough to handle.

Meanwhile, heat 1½ tablespoons of the butter in a small skillet over medium heat. Add the shallots and sauté for 4 to 5 minutes, until tender. Add the thyme and cook for 1 minute. Set aside.

Cut the potatoes in half lengthwise and carefully scoop out some of the warm potato into a medium bowl with a teaspoon, leaving a ½-inch-thick shell of sweet potato. The potatoes should look like little canoes. Sprinkle the potato shells generously with salt and pepper. Add the remaining 4 tablespoons of butter to the scooped-out potato flesh and mash it with a fork. Add the egg, shallots, Taleggio, ¾ teaspoon salt, and ¼ teaspoon pepper and stir until combined. Spoon the mixture into the sweet potato shells and top each with a sprig of fresh thyme. Bake for 20 to 30 minutes, until puffed and lightly browned. Serve hot.

MAKE IT AHEAD: Assemble the sweet potatoes and refrigerate them for up to 24 hours. Bake before serving.

dessert

Skillet Brownies

Coffee Granita

Salty Oatmeal Chocolate Chunk Cookies

Fresh Apple Spice Cake

Make-Ahead Whipped Cream

Chocolate Cake with Mocha Frosting

Tri-Berry Crumbles

Fresh Blueberry Pie

Dark Chocolate Terrine with Orange Sauce

Decadent (Gluten-Free!)
Chocolate Cake

Tres Leches Cake with Berries

Lemon Poppy Seed Cake

Lemon Ginger Molasses Cake

Make-Ahead Zabaglione
with Amaretti

Vanilla Semifreddo
with Raspberry Sauce

Salted Caramel Nuts

Ginger Shortbread

English Chocolate Crisps

the power of baking

I'm embarrassed to say, I think my husband fell in love with me because of the boxes of brownies I sent him when he was in college. It was just at that time in the late 1960s when the women's movement was getting started and all the smart women I knew were burning their bras and protesting the war in Vietnam. I, on the other hand, was baking brownies and sending them to my boyfriend in college. Now looking back, while it might have been an old-fashioned thing to do, I'm so glad I did it! To a college student eating awful dining hall food and spending late nights in the library, a box of homemade brownies must have looked like a gift from heaven. P.S. We've been married for 45 years, and I'm still making him brownies—now I bake them in a skillet and serve them warm!

Recently I heard another story about the power of baking. Sally Lee, the amazing editor in chief of *Ladies' Home Journal*, kindly invited me to lunch at the magazine. As we were eating, she told me a story about her mother, Dorothy Lee, who lives in a small village in the north of England. Dorothy was living on her own, so she decided to indulge her passion for baking to keep herself busy. The weather in that part of England is pretty bleak, and baking just seemed like a happy thing to do. As Sally wrote in her monthly magazine column, Dorothy "offers cake to the man who mows the lawn and to the woman who comes weekly to help her with the housework. The two lads who clean her windows (British folks get their windows cleaned at least once a month) take a break to have a homemade treat." People in Dorothy's village know they can always stop by for a proper cup of tea, a slice of cake, and warm conversation. The postman and schoolchildren on their way home all stop by for a cookie or piece of cake fresh from the oven. On slow days, Dorothy even bakes treats for the birds that perch in her garden. How wonderful is that? By baking every day—and sometimes twice a day!—she's given herself a happy purpose and connected with so many people in her community. Now that's the power of baking. The Lemon Ginger Molasses Cake on page 222 is one of Dorothy's favorite cakes.

When my dad wasn't well, I used to visit him every week at the nursing home where he lived. I think he knew who I was—or at least he made me feel as though he did—and I would arrive with his favorite dessert, homemade rice pudding with raisins. I will always remember the big smile on his face when I walked into the room. I'll never know if it was me or the rice pudding, but frankly, who cares? It made him very happy and that's all I need to know.

Skillet Brownies serves 4

The Standard Grill in New York City is an amazing restaurant. We were served warm brownies in individual skillets for dessert. When you make brownies, you need to cool them first so you can cut them in squares; but when they're cooked in a skillet, you can eat them hot right out of the oven.

The skillets I use measure 5 inches across on the top, 3½ inches across the bottom, and 1 inch deep.

¼ pound (1 stick) unsalted butter

4 ounces plus ½ cup Hershey's semisweet chocolate chips, divided

1½ ounces unsweetened chocolate

2 extra-large eggs

2 teaspoons instant coffee powder, such as Nescafé

1½ teaspoons pure vanilla extract

½ cup plus 1 tablespoon sugar

¼ cup plus 1 tablespoon all-purpose flour, divided

1 teaspoon baking powder

¼ teaspoon kosher salt

1 pint vanilla ice cream, such as Häagen-Dazs

Preheat the oven to 350 degrees.

Heat the butter, 4 ounces of the chocolate chips, and the unsweetened chocolate together in a medium heat-proof bowl set over simmering water just until the chocolate melts. Remove the bowl from the heat and allow to cool for 15 minutes. In a large bowl, stir (do not beat) together the eggs, coffee powder, vanilla, and sugar. Stir the chocolate mixture into the egg mixture and set aside to cool to room temperature.

In a medium bowl, sift together ¼ cup of the flour, the baking powder, and salt and stir it into the chocolate mixture. Toss the remaining ½ cup of chocolate chips and one tablespoon of flour together in a medium bowl and stir them into the chocolate mixture. Spoon the mixture into 4 individual cast-iron skillets (see note) and place them on a sheet pan. Bake for 22 minutes exactly. Don't overbake! A toothpick inserted in the center will not come out clean. Serve warm with a scoop of ice cream.

MAKE IT AHEAD: Prepare the batter and store covered in the refrigerator for a day. Spoon into skillets, smooth the tops, and bake.

Coffee Granita SERVES 6

Granita is an Italian ice, which is often made with water, sugar, and fruit juice or wine. I made this granita with coffee and coffee liqueur, and topped it off with a big dollop of whipped cream.

3 cups strong, hot brewed coffee, regular or decaf (see note)
¾ cup sugar
2 teaspoons coffee liqueur, such as Tia Maria
1 teaspoon pure vanilla extract
Make-Ahead Whipped Cream (page 197)

Be sure you use a pan with a flat bottom.

Combine the coffee, sugar, coffee liqueur, and vanilla and stir until the sugar dissolves. Pour the mixture into a 9 × 13-inch pan. Place the pan in the freezer for 1 hour, until the mixture starts to become slushy around the edges. Rake the mixture with a dinner fork to break up the crystals and place the pan back in the freezer. Every 30 minutes, rake the mixture, until it is completely frozen and granular throughout. Wrap well and keep frozen for a few hours, until ready to serve.

Spoon the granita into bowls or stemmed glasses, such as martini glasses, and top with a dollop of whipped cream. Serve immediately.

I use 4 cups water (using a measuring cup, not the markings on the coffeemaker) and ½ cup ground coffee to prepare the strong coffee.

MAKE IT AHEAD: Store the granita in the freezer for up to 3 hours.

Salty Oatmeal Chocolate Chunk Cookies

MAKES 28 TO 32 COOKIES

Oatmeal cookies or chocolate chunk cookies—which would my friends like best? How about both together? Some dried cranberries for tartness and a sprinkle of sea salt make these my all-time favorite cookies.

½ pound (2 sticks) unsalted butter, at room temperature
¾ cup light brown sugar, lightly packed
¾ cup granulated sugar
2 teaspoons pure vanilla extract
2 extra-large eggs, at room temperature
1¾ cups all-purpose flour
1 teaspoon baking soda
1 teaspoon kosher salt
1¼ cups old-fashioned oats, such as Quaker
¾ pound bittersweet chocolate, such as Lindt, chopped in chunks
¾ cup dried cranberries
Fleur de sel

If you prefer cookies thin and crisp, bake them straight from the mixing bowl. If you prefer them chewy in the middle and crisp outside, chill the balls of dough.

Preheat the oven to 375 degrees. Line 3 sheet pans with parchment paper.

In an electric mixer fitted with the paddle attachment, beat the butter, brown sugar, and granulated sugar on medium-high speed for 3 minutes, until light and fluffy. Scrape down the bowl with a rubber spatula. On low speed, add the vanilla, then the eggs, one at a time. Scrape down the bowl again.

Meanwhile, sift the flour, baking soda, and salt into a medium bowl. Mix in the oats. With the mixer on low, slowly add the flour mixture to the butter-sugar mixture. Don't overbeat it! With a rubber spatula, stir in the chocolate and cranberries until the dough is well mixed. With a 1¾-inch ice cream scoop (or two spoons), scoop round balls of dough onto the prepared sheet pans. Sprinkle lightly with fleur de sel. Bake for 10 to 12 minutes, until nicely browned. Serve warm or at room temperature.

MAKE IT AHEAD: Scoop balls of dough, place in sealed containers, and refrigerate for up to a week or freeze for up to 3 months. Defrost and bake before serving. Baked cookies can be stored in plastic bags and reheated for 5 minutes at 350 degrees.

Fresh Apple Spice Cake serves 9 to 12

This apple cake hits all the right notes—tart apples with brown sugar, orange zest, and lots of apple pie spices. I serve it with a scoop of vanilla ice cream and a drizzle of warm caramel sauce.

1 cup chopped pecans

½ cup dark rum, such as Mount Gay

1 cup golden raisins

1 cup granulated sugar

1 cup dark brown sugar, lightly packed

3 extra-large eggs, at room temperature

¾ cup vegetable oil

2 teaspoons pure vanilla extract

2 teaspoons grated orange zest (2 oranges)

2½ cups all-purpose flour

2 teaspoons baking powder

½ teaspoon kosher salt

2 teaspoons ground cinnamon

½ teaspoon ground nutmeg

½ teaspoon ground ginger

⅛ teaspoon ground cloves

1½ pounds Granny Smith apples, peeled, cored, and ¼-inch-diced (3 to 4 apples)

Vanilla ice cream, such as Häagen-Dazs

Caramel sauce, such as Fran's, heated

Preheat the oven to 350 degrees. Grease and flour a 9 × 13 × 2-inch baking pan.

Place the pecans on a sheet pan and toast them for 5 to 10 minutes, until lightly toasted. Set aside. Combine the rum and raisins in a small bowl, cover with plastic wrap, and microwave for 60 seconds. Set aside.

In the bowl of an electric mixer fitted with the paddle attachment, beat the granulated sugar, brown sugar, eggs, vegetable oil, vanilla, and orange zest on medium speed for 3 minutes. Sift the flour, baking powder, salt, cinnamon, nutmeg, ginger, and

MAKE IT AHEAD: Bake and store at room temperature for up to 24 hours.

cloves into a medium bowl. With the mixer on low, slowly add the flour mixture to the wet mixture, just until combined. Drain the raisins, discarding the liquid. With a rubber spatula, fold the raisins, pecans, and apples into the batter. Spread into the prepared pan and smooth the top.

Bake for 35 to 40 minutes, until a toothpick inserted in the center comes out clean. Set aside to cool, cut into squares, and serve warm or at room temperature with a scoop of vanilla ice cream and a drizzle of warm caramel sauce.

Make-Ahead Whipped Cream

One of the things everyone thinks you need to make at the last minute is
whipped cream. In fact, if you add just a little crème fraîche to stabilize
the cream, you can actually make it a few hours ahead. By the way, if you
accidentally overwhip the cream, just add a splash of cream to the bowl and
give it a quick beat. It will form soft peaks again.

1½ cups cold heavy cream
¼ cup confectioners' sugar
2 tablespoons granulated sugar
2 tablespoons crème fraîche
1 teaspoon pure vanilla extract

MAKE IT AHEAD: Refrigerate
in a sealed container for up
to 4 hours.

Place the cream, confectioners' sugar,
granulated sugar, crème fraîche,
and vanilla in the bowl of an electric
mixer fitted with the whisk attachment. Beat on high speed, until it
forms soft peaks. Serve cold.

Chocolate Cake with Mocha Frosting SERVES 12

The original purpose for icing a cake was to keep it moist for days, which is a good make-ahead tip. You can make this rich chocolate cake in advance or bake the cake, freeze it, and then make the frosting the day you want to serve it. Either way, your guests will be very happy!

12 tablespoons (1½ sticks) unsalted butter, at room
    temperature
2 cups sugar
1 tablespoon pure vanilla extract
3 extra-large eggs, at room temperature
1¾ cups all-purpose flour
1 teaspoon baking soda
1 teaspoon kosher salt
⅔ cup hottest tap water
⅔ cup unsweetened cocoa powder, such as Pernigotti
1 teaspoon instant espresso powder
⅔ cup half-and-half
Mocha Frosting (recipe follows)

Preheat the oven to 350 degrees. Grease a 9 × 13 × 2-inch baking pan. Line with parchment paper, then grease and flour the pan.

Place the butter and sugar in the bowl of an electric mixer fitted with the paddle attachment and beat on medium speed for 4 to 5 minutes, until light and fluffy, scraping down the bowl. On medium speed, add the vanilla, then beat in the eggs, one at a time, until incorporated and the batter is smooth.

Sift the flour, baking soda, and salt together in a medium bowl. In another bowl or a liquid measuring cup, whisk together the hot water, cocoa powder, and espresso powder until smooth. Add the half-and-half and whisk until smooth. With the mixer on low, add the flour and chocolate mixtures alternately in thirds, starting and ending with the flour. With a rubber spatula, scrape down the bowl to be sure the batter is well mixed. Pour the

MAKE IT AHEAD: Prepare the cake with frosting and leave at room temperature for up to 6 hours. The cake alone can be frozen for up to 2 months. Frost before serving.

batter into the prepared pan, smooth the top, and bake for 25 to 35 minutes, until a cake tester inserted in the center comes out clean. Cool completely in the pan. Turn out onto a flat platter or board and frost the top with the mocha frosting. Cut in squares and serve.

Mocha Frosting FROSTS ONE 9 × 13-INCH CAKE

12 ounces bittersweet chocolate, such as Lindt, ¼-inch-chopped
3 tablespoons unsalted butter, diced, at room temperature
2 teaspoons instant espresso powder
1¼ cups heavy cream
1 tablespoon Kahlúa
1 teaspoon pure vanilla extract

Place the chocolate, butter, and espresso powder in a bowl. Heat the cream to simmer and pour it over the chocolate mixture, stirring occasionally, until the chocolate is melted. (If the chocolate isn't melted, microwave the mixture for 15 seconds.) Stir in the Kahlúa and vanilla and stir until the mixture is smooth. Cover and refrigerate for 30 minutes only, until cool but not cold.

Scrape down the bowl and beat the frosting with a handheld mixer on high speed for 15 to 20 seconds *only,* until the mixture forms soft peaks. (If you overbeat it, it will curdle!) Spread on the cake immediately with a metal spatula.

Tri-Berry Crumbles SERVES 6

There's something wonderful about having your own dessert, so I made these crumbles in the small dishes that I usually use for crèmes brûlées. It's the perfect combination of warm, juicy berries and crunchy oatmeal topping.

2 cups fresh blueberries (12 ounces)

2½ cups fresh raspberries (18 ounces)

2 cups fresh strawberries, halved, or quartered if large

½ cup granulated sugar

3 tablespoons cornstarch

1½ teaspoons grated lemon zest (2 lemons)

3 tablespoons freshly squeezed lemon juice

FOR THE CRUMBLE

¾ cup all-purpose flour

¾ cup granulated sugar

½ cup light brown sugar, lightly packed

½ cup old-fashioned oats, such as Quaker

¾ teaspoon ground cinnamon

¾ teaspoon kosher salt

¼ pound (1 stick) unsalted butter, diced, at room temperature

Vanilla ice cream, for serving

Preheat the oven to 350 degrees. Place 6 crème brûlée dishes on a sheet pan lined with parchment paper.

In a large bowl, toss together the blueberries, raspberries, strawberries, ½ cup granulated sugar, the cornstarch, lemon zest, and lemon juice. Divide the mixture evenly among the crème brûlée dishes, including any juices that collect.

For the crumble, combine the flour, ¾ cup granulated sugar, the brown sugar, oats, cinnamon, and salt in the bowl of an electric mixer fitted with the paddle attachment. Add the butter and mix it on low speed until the mixture is crumbly. Pinch it with your fingers until it makes large crumbles and distribute it on the berries (it will not cover them entirely). Bake for 35 to 40 minutes, until the juices are bubbly and the topping is browned. Serve warm with a small scoop of vanilla ice cream.

MAKE IT AHEAD: Assemble the crumbles, refrigerate for up to 4 hours, and bake before serving.

Fresh Blueberry Pie makes one 9-inch pie; serves 6

Recently, I was looking through some old notebooks of recipes that we used at my specialty food store. I came across this blueberry pie recipe and I was surprised to see that even decades ago, I was using Cassis and lemon zest to bring out the flavor of the blueberries.

4 cups (20 ounces) fresh blueberries, washed and dried
½ cup sugar, plus extra for sprinkling
½ cup all-purpose flour
1 teaspoon grated lemon zest
¼ cup freshly squeezed lemon juice (2 lemons)
1 tablespoon Cassis liqueur
Perfect Pie Crusts (recipe follows)
1 egg beaten with 1 tablespoon milk or cream, for egg wash

Preheat the oven to 400 degrees. Line a sheet pan with parchment paper.

Mix the blueberries, ½ cup of sugar, the flour, lemon zest, lemon juice, and Cassis in a large bowl. Carefully ease one pie crust into a 9-inch pie plate, making sure not to stretch the dough, or it will shrink as the pie bakes. With a sharp knife, cut the excess dough off at the edge of the pie plate. Spoon the blueberry mixture into the pie shell, scraping the bowl with a rubber spatula to be sure you include all the juices.

Brush the edge of the crust with the egg wash. Carefully lay the second crust on top, again easing—not stretching—it onto the pie. Cut the excess dough off at the edge of the pie plate. Press the two edges together with a dinner fork. Brush the top crust with the egg wash, cut three slits for steam to escape, and sprinkle with sugar.

Place the pie on the prepared sheet pan and bake in the middle of the oven for 45 to 50 minutes, until the filling is very bubbly and the crust is nicely browned. Allow to cool and serve warm or at room temperature.

MAKE IT AHEAD: Bake the pie up to 24 hours in advance. Reheat for 10 minutes at 350 degrees and serve warm or at room temperature.

Perfect Pie Crusts makes two 9-inch crusts

There are three secrets to perfect pie crust. First, the butter, shortening, and water must all be very cold. Second, let the dough sit in the refrigerator for 30 minutes before rolling; and finally, don't stretch the dough when you're placing it into the pan.

12 tablespoons (1½ sticks) very cold unsalted butter
3 cups all-purpose flour
1 tablespoon sugar
1 teaspoon kosher salt
⅓ cup very cold vegetable shortening, such as Crisco, diced
½ cup ice water

Cut the butter in ½-inch dice and return it to the refrigerator while you prepare the flour mixture. Place the flour, sugar, and salt in the bowl of a food processor fitted with the steel blade and pulse a few times to mix. Add the butter and shortening and pulse 10 to 12 times, until the butter is the size of peas. With the machine running, pour the ice water down the feed tube and pulse the machine until the dough begins to form a ball. Dump the dough out on a floured board and turn it into a ball. Wrap it in plastic wrap and refrigerate for 30 minutes.

Cut the dough in half. Roll each piece out on a well-floured board into a 12- to 13-inch circle, rolling from the center to the edge, turning and flouring the dough to make sure it doesn't stick to the board.

MAKE IT AHEAD: Prepare the dough, form into 2 balls, wrap well, and refrigerate for up to 4 days or freeze for up to 3 months. Defrost in the refrigerator.

Dark Chocolate Terrine
with Orange Sauce SERVES 10

This recipe was inspired by two similar recipes—one from Thomas Keller's French Laundry and one from the restaurant Taillevent in Paris. I've paired it with a fragrant Grand Marnier orange sauce and some flaked sea salt to make it even better!

Vegetable oil, for greasing the pan
½ pound (2 sticks) unsalted butter
12 ounces bittersweet chocolate, such as Lindt, broken
   in bits
1 teaspoon instant coffee powder
1 cup sifted confectioners' sugar
⅓ cup unsweetened cocoa powder, such as Pernigotti
8 extra-large egg yolks, at room temperature
1 tablespoon Cognac or brandy
Pinch of kosher salt
3 extra-large egg whites, at room temperature
1 tablespoon granulated sugar
½ cup cold heavy cream
1 teaspoon pure vanilla extract
Orange Sauce (recipe follows)
Freshly grated orange zest, for serving
Fleur de sel, for serving

A hot, dry knife makes cutting easier. You can put it under a hot tap and then dry it—or hold the knife briefly over an open flame on the stove.

Lightly oil an 8½ × 4½ × 2-inch loaf pan and line it as neatly as possible with plastic wrap, allowing the ends to drape over the sides. (I lay two pieces of plastic wrap crosswise in the pan, overlapping in the center.) Place the pan in the freezer.

   Place a large heat-proof bowl over a pan of simmering water. Place the butter in the bowl, then the chocolate and coffee powder and heat until just melted, stirring occasionally with a rubber spatula. As soon as the chocolate and butter are melted, take the bowl off the heat and whisk in, one at a time, and *in order,* first the confectioners' sugar, then the cocoa powder, egg yolks, Cognac, and salt. Set the bowl aside for 15 minutes to cool.

MAKE IT AHEAD: Prepare the terrine and refrigerate for up to a week. Make the orange sauce and refrigerate for up to 5 days.

Place the egg whites and granulated sugar in the bowl of an electric mixer fitted with the whisk attachment and beat on high speed until the whites form firm but not dry peaks. Fold the whites into the cooled chocolate mixture with a rubber spatula.

Without cleaning the bowl or whisk attachment, pour the cream and vanilla into the bowl and beat on high speed until it forms firm peaks. Fold the cream carefully but thoroughly into the chocolate mixture. Pour into the prepared loaf pan, smooth the top, fold the plastic wrap over the top, and chill for 4 hours or overnight.

To serve, turn the terrine out of the mold and unwrap it. Spoon a puddle of Orange Sauce in the middle of each dessert plate and place a slice of the terrine in the middle. Sprinkle each serving lightly with orange zest and fleur de sel.

Orange Sauce MAKES 2 CUPS

4 extra-large egg yolks, at room temperature (see note)

½ cup sugar

1 teaspoon cornstarch

1¾ cups scalded whole milk (see note)

1 teaspoon pure vanilla extract

1½ teaspoons Cognac or brandy

1 tablespoon Grand Marnier liqueur

¼ teaspoon grated orange zest

Beat the egg yolks and sugar in the bowl of an electric mixer fitted with the paddle attachment on medium-high speed for 3 minutes, until very thick. Reduce to low speed and mix in the cornstarch.

With the mixer still on low, slowly pour the hot milk into the egg mixture (I use a liquid measuring cup for pouring). Pour the mixture into a clean, small, deep saucepan and cook over medium-low heat, stirring constantly with a wooden spoon, until it reaches 180 degrees on a candy thermometer and thickens to the consistency of heavy cream. The mixture will coat the spoon. Don't cook it above 180 degrees or the eggs will scramble! Immediately (it will keep cooking in the saucepan), pour the sauce through a fine-mesh sieve into a bowl and stir in the vanilla, Cognac, Grand Marnier, and orange zest. Cover and chill.

It's perfectly safe to leave eggs at room temperature overnight; the shell protects them from bacteria.

To scald milk, heat it to just below the boiling point. You'll see bubbles forming around the edge.

Decadent (Gluten-Free!) Chocolate Cake SERVES 8 TO 10

This cake is gluten-free but no one will suspect because the cake and ganache are so rich and fudgy. Thomas Keller's Cup 4 Cup gluten-free flour is pure genius.

1 pound plus 3 ounces bittersweet chocolate such as Lindt, broken into chunks

10 tablespoons (1¼ sticks) unsalted butter, cut into pieces, at room temperature

1 tablespoon Cup 4 Cup gluten-free flour

1½ tablespoons sugar

1 teaspoon instant coffee granules

¼ teaspoon kosher salt

4 extra-large eggs, at room temperature, separated

¼ cup heavy cream

Coffee or vanilla ice cream, for serving

You can certainly make this with 1 tablespoon all-purpose flour instead of gluten-free flour.

Preheat the oven to 425 degrees. Grease an 8-inch springform pan and line the bottom with parchment paper.

Place the one pound of chocolate in a large heat-proof bowl set over a pan of simmering water and stir occasionally until the chocolate is melted. Off the heat, immediately stir in the butter, flour, sugar, coffee granules, and salt with a rubber spatula. Whisk in the egg yolks until smooth.

Place the egg whites in the bowl of an electric mixer fitted with the whisk attachment and beat until they form soft peaks. Scrape the egg whites into the chocolate mixture and fold them in very carefully with a rubber spatula, just until combined. Scrape the mixture into the prepared pan, smooth the top, and bake for 15 minutes exactly. (Be sure your oven temperature is accurate!)

Turn the oven off and leave the cake in the oven, leaving the door slightly ajar. Allow the cake to cool in the oven for 1 hour. The cake will sink in the middle.

Carefully release the sides of the pan and slide the cake onto a flat serving plate or cake stand. Place the 3 ounces of chocolate

MAKE IT AHEAD: Prepare the cake and allow it to sit at room temperature for up to 6 hours.

and the heavy cream in a heat-proof bowl set over a pan of simmering water and heat just until the chocolate melts, stirring occasionally. Add a drop of cream if the mixture is too thick to pour. Pour the chocolate onto the sunken part of the cake, leaving the edge unfrosted. Allow to cool and serve warm or at room temperature with a scoop
of ice cream.

Tres Leches Cake with Berries SERVES 9 TO 12

*This is the most unassuming cake but it's so much better than you expect—
something between a cake and a pudding. I serve it with mixed berries and
a dollop of whipped cream. This is the dessert of your dreams.*

1½ cups all-purpose flour

2 teaspoons baking powder

¾ teaspoon kosher salt

3 extra-large eggs, at room temperature

1 cup plus 5 tablespoons granulated sugar

2 teaspoons pure vanilla extract

½ cup whole milk

1¼ cups heavy cream

1 (12-ounce) can evaporated milk

1 (14-ounce) can sweetened condensed milk

½ teaspoon pure almond extract

Seeds scraped from 1 vanilla bean

8 cups mixed fresh raspberries and sliced strawberries,
    for serving

Sifted confectioners' sugar, for dusting

Make-Ahead Whipped Cream (page 197)

Preheat the oven to 350 degrees. Butter a 9 × 13 × 2-inch baking
pan.

Sift the flour, baking powder, and salt into a small bowl and
set aside. Place the eggs, 1 cup of granulated sugar, and the
vanilla in the bowl of an electric mixer fitted with the paddle
attachment and beat on medium-high speed for 10 minutes
(really!) until light yellow and fluffy. Reduce the speed to low and
slowly add half the flour mixture, then the milk, and finally the
remaining flour mixture. Mix with a rubber spatula to be sure
the batter is well mixed. Pour the batter into the prepared pan,
smooth the top, and bake for 25 minutes, until the cake springs
back when touched lightly in the middle and a cake tester comes
out clean. Set aside to cool in the pan for 30 minutes.

In a 4-cup liquid measuring cup, whisk together the heavy
cream, evaporated milk, sweetened condensed milk, almond

MAKE IT AHEAD: Prepare the
cake completely and refrigerate
for up to 5 days. Serve with the
berries and whipped cream.

extract, and vanilla seeds. Using a bamboo skewer, poke holes all over the cooled cake and slowly pour the cream mixture over the cake, allowing it to be absorbed completely before continuing to pour on more of the mixture. Cover the cake with plastic wrap and refrigerate for at least 6 hours.

To serve, toss the fruit with the 5 tablespoons of granulated sugar. Dust the cake with confectioners' sugar, cut in squares, and place on dessert plates. Surround the cake with the fruit, put a dollop of whipped cream on top, and serve.

Lemon Poppy Seed Cake   SERVES 10 TO 12

There's a wonderful old-fashioned quality to lemon poppy seed cake but the challenge is to make one that's really flavorful and moist. Mine is baked with lots of freshly squeezed lemon juice and zest plus a lemon syrup that soaks into the cake.

1 cup buttermilk, shaken

⅓ cup poppy seeds (1.75 ounces)

Nonstick baking spray with flour, such as Baker's Joy

½ pound (2 sticks) unsalted butter, at room temperature

2½ cups granulated sugar, divided

4 extra-large eggs, at room temperature

1 teaspoon pure vanilla extract

⅓ cup grated lemon zest, loosely packed (4 to 5 large lemons)

2¾ cups all-purpose flour

¼ cup cornstarch

1 teaspoon kosher salt

½ teaspoon baking powder

½ teaspoon baking soda

¾ cup freshly squeezed lemon juice, divided

FOR THE GLAZE

1 cup sifted confectioners' sugar

1½ tablespoons freshly squeezed lemon juice

Pour the buttermilk into a 2-cup liquid measuring cup, stir in the poppy seeds, and set aside at room temperature for at least 2 hours.

Preheat the oven to 350 degrees. Thoroughly spray the inside of a Bundt pan with the baking spray and set aside.

In the bowl of an electric mixer fitted with the paddle attachment, cream the butter and 2 cups of the granulated sugar on medium speed for about 5 minutes, until light yellow and fluffy. With the mixer on low, add the eggs, one at a time, the vanilla, and lemon zest, scraping down the bowl with a rubber spatula.

Sift the flour, cornstarch, salt, baking powder, and baking soda into a medium bowl. Add ¼ cup of the lemon juice to the

MAKE IT AHEAD: Bake the cake and spoon the syrup over it. Wrap and refrigerate for up to 3 days. Glaze and serve at room temperature.

buttermilk mixture. With the mixer on low speed, alternately add the flour mixture and buttermilk mixture in thirds, beginning and ending with the flour. Scrape the bowl with a rubber spatula to be sure the batter is well mixed. Spoon the batter into the prepared pan, smooth the top, and bake for 40 to 50 minutes, until a cake tester comes out clean.

Meanwhile, place the remaining ½ cup of granulated sugar and the remaining ½ cup of lemon juice in a small saucepan and cook over high heat until the sugar dissolves. Set aside. When the cake is done, allow it to cool in the pan for 10 minutes, then turn it out onto a baking rack set over a large plate. Spoon the warm lemon syrup slowly over the cake, allowing it to be absorbed into the cake. Set aside for at least 30 minutes to cool.

For the glaze, whisk the confectioners' sugar and lemon juice together in a small bowl, adding a little more sugar or lemon juice to make a smooth, thick, but pourable glaze. Drizzle over the cake, allowing it to drip down the sides. Transfer to a flat cake plate and serve at room temperature.

Lemon Ginger Molasses Cake serves 8

Dorothy Lee is the mother of Sally Lee, the editor in chief of Ladies' Home
Journal. *This recipe is inspired by Sally's favorite cake that her mother
bakes for anyone who might be stopping by for a cup of tea and an afternoon
chat. It's old-fashioned, English, and so delicious!*

*Crystallized ginger is dried,
not in syrup.*

¼ pound (1 stick) unsalted butter, at room temperature
½ cup light brown sugar, lightly packed
2 extra-large eggs, at room temperature
½ cup unsulphured molasses
2 teaspoons grated lemon zest, plus extra for serving
1½ cups all-purpose flour
2 teaspoons ground ginger
½ teaspoon baking soda
½ teaspoon kosher salt
½ cup whole milk
⅓ cup small-diced crystallized ginger, plus extra for serving
Make-Ahead Whipped Cream (page 197), for serving

Preheat the oven to 350 degrees. Grease an 8-inch round baking
pan, line with parchment paper, then grease and flour the pan.

In the bowl of an electric mixer fitted with the paddle attachment, cream the butter and sugar on medium speed for 3 to
5 minutes, until light and fluffy. Scrape down the sides with a
rubber spatula. Add the eggs, one at a time, the molasses, and the
2 teaspoons of lemon zest and mix until combined. (The batter
may look curdled.)

Sift together the flour, ginger, baking soda, and salt. With the
mixer on low, slowly add the dry ingredients alternately with the
milk, scraping down the sides. Mix until smooth. With a rubber
spatula, fold in the ⅓ cup of crystallized ginger.

Pour the batter into the prepared pan, smooth the top, and
bake for 30 to 35 minutes, until a toothpick *just* comes out
clean. Don't overbake it! Cool in the pan for 30 minutes, turn
out onto a baking rack, and cool completely. Spread the top with
whipped cream and sprinkle with crystallized ginger and grated
lemon zest.

MAKE IT AHEAD: Prepare
the cake, wrap tightly, and
refrigerate for up to 1 day.
Garnish with whipped cream,
ginger, and lemon zest.

Make-Ahead Zabaglione with Amaretti SERVES 4 TO 5

One of the great desserts of Italy is zabaglione, an ethereal warm custard made by whisking egg yolks together with Marsala wine over simmering water. Unfortunately, it needs to be prepared just before serving, which is a problem. Instead, I make this cold zabaglione with whipped cream and crushed amaretti that's even better made ahead.

6 extra-large egg yolks
½ cup superfine sugar
¾ cup *dry* Italian Marsala wine, such as Florio
½ teaspoon pure vanilla extract
¼ teaspoon pure almond extract
¾ cup cold heavy cream
4 to 6 (double) Italian Amaretti di Saronno cookies, lightly
  crushed (see note)

Amaretti di Saronno come 2 in each wrapper; I use the cookies from 4 to 6 wrappers. Crush them lightly with the side of a knife blade.

Place the egg yolks, sugar, and Marsala wine in a large heat-proof glass bowl and whisk them together. Place the bowl on a pan of simmering water to make a double boiler and whisk the mixture almost constantly for 5 to 7 minutes, until it expands in volume and becomes thickened. You'll see the froth disappear and the whisk will leave a little trail in the mixture. Don't walk away from it or you'll end up with scrambled eggs! Off the heat, whisk in the vanilla and almond extracts. Set aside for 30 minutes to cool to room temperature, whisking once or twice as it cools.

Place the cream in the bowl of an electric mixer fitted with the whisk attachment (you can also use a hand mixer) and beat it just until it forms firm peaks. With a rubber spatula, carefully fold the cream into the Marsala mixture. Spoon half of the mixture into each of 4 or 5 decorative glasses (depending on the size), sprinkle each with 1 tablespoon of crushed Amaretti, and spoon the rest of the mixture on top. Sprinkle with the remaining Amaretti crumbs, cover with plastic wrap, and chill for a few hours or overnight. Serve cold.

MAKE IT AHEAD: Prepare completely and refrigerate for up to 2 days. Sprinkle on extra crushed Amaretti before serving.

Vanilla Semifreddo with Raspberry Sauce SERVES 8

This dessert is a frozen vanilla mousse (semifreddo means "half-frozen" in Italian) that's served on a puddle of fresh raspberry sauce. Heaven!

Vegetable oil, for greasing the pan
4 extra-large eggs, separated, at room temperature
½ cup sugar, divided
Seeds scraped from ½ vanilla bean
½ teaspoon cream of tartar
1 cup cold heavy cream
1 tablespoon vanilla liqueur, such as Navan (optional)
1 teaspoon pure vanilla extract
Fresh Raspberry Sauce (recipe follows)
Fresh raspberries, for serving

Lightly oil an 8½ × 4½ × 2-inch loaf pan and line it as neatly as possible with plastic wrap, allowing enough to drape over the sides to later cover the top. (I lay two pieces of plastic wrap across the pan, overlapping in the middle.) Place the pan in the freezer.

Put the egg yolks (reserve ⅓ cup of the egg whites and discard or save the rest for another use), ¼ cup of the sugar, and the vanilla seeds in a medium heat-proof bowl and beat with a handheld mixer fitted with the beater attachment for 2 minutes, until light yellow and thickened. Place the bowl over a pan of simmering water and beat the mixture continually for 3 minutes, until doubled in volume and warm to the touch. Off the heat, beat the mixture for one minute.

In the bowl of an electric mixer fitted with the whisk attachment, add the reserved egg whites, the remaining ¼ cup of sugar, and the cream of tartar and beat on high speed until the whites form firm but not dry peaks. Fold the egg whites into the egg mixture with a rubber spatula.

Without washing the mixer or whisk, pour the heavy cream, vanilla liqueur (if using), and vanilla into the bowl and beat on high speed until it forms soft peaks. Fold the whipped cream

MAKE IT AHEAD: Prepare the semifreddo and freeze for up to 1 month. Prepare the raspberry sauce and refrigerate for up to a week or freeze for up to 3 months.

carefully but thoroughly into the egg mixture. Pour the mixture into the prepared pan, cover with plastic wrap, and freeze for at least 4 hours.

To unmold, dip the pan in a bowl of hot tap water for 8 to 10 seconds and turn the semifreddo upside down onto a rectangular serving plate. Peel off the plastic wrap. (You can cover and refreeze the semifreddo for a few hours on the serving plate.) Pour several tablespoons of raspberry sauce on each dessert plate, cut 1-inch-thick slices of the semifreddo, and place them in the center of the sauce. Sprinkle each serving with raspberries, and serve immediately.

Fresh Raspberry Sauce MAKES 1½ CUPS

1 half-pint fresh raspberries (6 ounces)
½ cup sugar
½ cup good raspberry preserves (6 ounces)
1 tablespoon framboise liqueur

Place the raspberries, sugar, and ¼ cup water in a small saucepan. Bring to a boil, lower the heat, and simmer for 4 minutes. Pour the mixture and the preserves into the bowl of a food processor fitted with the steel blade and process until smooth. Stir in the framboise and chill.

Salted Caramel Nuts MAKES 8 CUPS

I tested these caramel nuts before a dinner party and I left a container on the counter to see if anyone noticed them. All evening, people would wander into the kitchen, open the container, take some, and put the lid back on. And then wander back into the kitchen again. They're irresistible!

1 cup *each* whole roasted salted cashews,
    whole large pecan halves, whole unsalted almonds,
    and whole walnut halves (4 cups total)
1½ cups sugar
2 teaspoons pure vanilla extract
2 teaspoons kosher salt
1 teaspoon fleur de sel

Preheat the oven to 350 degrees.

Combine the nuts on a sheet pan, spread them out, and roast them for 7 minutes, until they become fragrant. Set aside to cool.

After the nuts are cooled, place the sugar and ¼ cup of water in a medium (10-inch) sauté pan and mix with a fork until all of the sugar is moistened. Cook over medium-high heat until the sugar melts—from this point on, don't stir the caramel, swirl the pan! Don't worry—the mixture may look as though it's crystallizing. Continue to cook for 5 to 10 minutes, until the mixture becomes a clear golden brown, swirling the pan constantly at the end. (Careful—the caramel is very hot!) Off the heat, quickly add the vanilla (it will bubble up!) and swirl the pan to combine. Working quickly (the caramel will continue to cook in the pan), add the nuts and the kosher salt and toss with 2 large spoons until the nuts are completely coated.

Pour the nuts and any extra caramel in the pan onto a sheet pan lined with parchment paper. Spread the nuts out in one layer, pulling them apart with two forks. Sprinkle with the fleur de sel and set aside to cool. When they're completely cooled, carefully break the nuts into large clusters with your hands, trying not to break the nuts too much.

MAKE IT AHEAD: Prepare completely and store in sealed containers at room temperature for up to a week.

Ginger Shortbread MAKES 20 TO 24 COOKIES

I adore the shortbread at E.A.T. on Madison Avenue in New York City. Eli Zabar, the owner, was kind enough to share his recipe. I added crystallized ginger and ended up with a really sophisticated cookie that's both spicy and sweet. It's great for dessert with a bowl of vanilla ice cream.

I find the edges of the shortbread are ever so slightly sharper if you chill the cookies for 10 minutes before you bake them.

¾ pound (3 sticks) unsalted butter, at room temperature
1 cup sugar, plus extra for sprinkling
1 teaspoon pure vanilla extract
3½ cups all-purpose flour
1 teaspoon kosher salt
¾ cup minced crystallized ginger (not in syrup)

Preheat the oven to 350 degrees.

In the bowl of an electric mixer fitted with the paddle attachment, mix the butter and 1 cup of sugar on medium-low speed, just until they are combined. (Don't whip!) Add the vanilla and 2 teaspoons water and mix until combined. In a medium bowl, sift together the flour and salt. With the mixer on low, slowly add the flour mixture to the butter mixture and mix until the dough starts to come together. Add the ginger, then dump onto a surface generously dusted with flour and shape into a flat disk. Wrap in plastic and chill for 30 minutes.

Roll the dough ⅜ inch thick and cut circles with a 2¾-inch plain round cookie cutter. Place the cookies on an ungreased baking sheet and sprinkle with sugar. Bake for 20 to 25 minutes, until the edges start to brown.

Cool to room temperature and serve.

MAKE IT AHEAD: Cut out the cookies, place in sealed containers, and refrigerate for up to a week or freeze for up to 3 months. Bake before serving.

English Chocolate Crisps MAKES 8 LARGE CRISPS

When I travel, I visit specialty food stores and bakeries to see what other people are up to. In London, a chocolate shop in Notting Hill called Melt makes these chocolate crisps. They're surprisingly simple: cornflakes coated in good chocolate! You don't taste the cereal; it just gives the chocolate an incredible crunch.

7¼ ounces milk chocolate, such as Perugina
5½ ounces bittersweet chocolate, such as Lindt or Perugina
3 cups cornflakes, such as Kellogg's
⅓ cup dried cranberries

Chop the two chocolates and place ¾ of them in a heat-proof bowl. Place the bowl in a microwave on high heat for 30 seconds, remove the bowl, and stir the chocolates vigorously with a wooden spoon. Continue heating and stirring the chocolates in 30-second intervals, switching to 15-second intervals as the chocolates start to melt, continuing to stir vigorously with a wooden spoon in between each heating. Heat only until the chocolates are just melted. Add the remaining quarter of the chocolates and stir vigorously until melted and smooth. (If the chocolate isn't completely melted, microwave it for another 5 or 10 seconds.)

Place the cornflakes in a medium bowl, pour the chocolate mixture over the cornflakes, and immediately fold them together with a rubber spatula, being careful not to break up the cornflakes. You'll want to work quickly so the chocolate doesn't harden. Fold in the cranberries.

Line a sheet pan with parchment paper. Working with 2 soup spoons, spoon 8 mounds of chocolate crisps onto the paper. Set aside at room temperature to cool completely until hardened. Peel the crisps off the paper and serve.

MAKE IT AHEAD: Allow the crisps to cool completely, then store for up to 5 days in a tightly sealed plastic bag or container at room temperature.

Sour Cream Corn Bread

Breakfast Ricotta
with Berries & Maple Syrup

Maple Vanilla Cream of Wheat

Overnight Belgian Waffles

Strawberry Rhubarb Compote
with Greek Yogurt

Mini Italian Frittatas

Make-Ahead Salt & Pepper Biscuits

Blueberry Bran Muffins

Raspberry Baked French Toast

Chocolate Banana Crumb Cake

Lee Bailey

Lee Bailey is one of my original style icons. In the 1970s, Jeffrey and I lived in Washington, D.C., and when we visited New York, we'd always go to Henri Bendel, which was then on 57th Street, where Lee had a store called Bailey-Huebner. The store carried amazingly beautiful modern tableware and it's where I discovered

large white platters for the first time. Looking at Lee's gorgeous platters, it occurred to me that instead of serving dinner in lots of small bowls as I used to do, I could create a more fun, dramatic dinner by arranging a rack of lamb down the middle of a large white oval platter with the roasted tomatoes on one side and the couscous on the other side. Now, that looked like a party! It was such a revelation that every time I went to New York City, I bought another big white serving dish from Lee, until all of a sudden I had a big stack of them.

Later, when I got to know Lee, I asked him what he thought the key to his style was. He told me that his great friend Liz Smith used to buy little vegetable brushes from him, and one time she asked if they came in any other color besides white. "Yes!" Lee said to her. "They come in tangerine, lemon yellow, and bright blue. But *here,* they only come in white!" Lee's secret was simplicity. Everything he sold was simple and elegant and I've followed his vision ever since.

The incomparable Nora Ephron was a great friend of Lee's and decades ago, she wrote an article about him in the *New York Times Magazine* that I've loved so much it's stayed on my desk ever since. She wrote:

When I first met [Lee], he was a designer, and he lived in one of those places you walked into and wanted to live in; everyone felt this way. Every single object in it was simple and beautiful. The glasses were beautiful. The seersucker napkins were beautiful, and what's more, they didn't have to be ironed. Everything was white, or beige, or sometimes gray. In fact, Geraldine Stutz [the head of Bendel's] walked into Lee's apartment and wanted to live in it so badly that she hired him to open a small shop at Henri Bendel's. Soon everything I owned was white or beige or sometimes gray.

Lee was also the perfect host. When you arrived at his house, he was always totally relaxed, as though nothing were going on. The table was set and Lee would serve a cocktail and something to nibble on, like a bowl of fresh peas. At some point, the party would move to the kitchen, where there was a little cutting and chopping—but not much—and suddenly, dinner was served. Lee's food was a little Southern, as he was, and it was always delicious. He cooked because he loved to bring people together, which is another reason why he was so influential in my life. He taught me that when you cook, your friends show up, and it's this philosophy that continues to fuel my love of cooking and entertaining. Lee also started the whole genre of what we call "lifestyle cookbooks" and was the person who sent me to Clarkson Potter, where I have been so happy for the past 15 years.

The Make-Ahead Salt & Pepper Biscuits on page 255 are inspired by Lee's Southern biscuits and are my tribute to him. Sadly, he's no longer with us, but I sure would like to make them for him right now.

Sour Cream Corn Bread makes 2 loaves

This all-American quick bread is usually served with dinner. To make it ahead, I bake it in loaves, and then slice, toast, and slather it with butter and jam for breakfast. Bob's Red Mill cornmeal is widely available and essential for this recipe.

½ pound (2 sticks) unsalted butter, melted, plus extra
    to grease the pan
3 cups all-purpose flour
1 cup Bob's Red Mill medium-grind yellow cornmeal
½ cup sugar
2 tablespoons baking powder (see note)
1 tablespoon kosher salt
1¼ cups whole milk
¾ cup sour cream
2 extra-large eggs, at room temperature
Salted butter and strawberry jam, for serving

Preheat the oven to 350 degrees. Grease and line the bottom of two 8½ × 4½ × 2-inch loaf pans with parchment paper.

Whisk together the flour, cornmeal, sugar, baking powder, and salt in a large bowl. In a separate bowl, whisk together the milk, sour cream, and eggs and then slowly whisk in the melted butter. Pour the wet ingredients into the dry ones and mix them together with a rubber spatula, until combined. Don't overmix! Pour the batter into the prepared pans, smooth the top, and bake for 35 to 40 minutes, until a toothpick comes out clean. Place the pans on a rack and cool completely.

When ready to serve, slice the corn bread, toast it, and serve with salted butter and strawberry jam.

Check the expiration date of your baking powder to make sure it's still active.

MAKE IT AHEAD: Bake the corn breads, cool completely, wrap tightly, and refrigerate for up to 4 days or freeze for up to 3 months. Defrost, if necessary, slice ½ inch thick, and toast.

Breakfast Ricotta with Berries & Maple Syrup SERVES 3 OR 4

I have Irish oatmeal and coffee for breakfast every weekday morning, so on the weekends I like to make something different. Homemade ricotta is delicious. I've mixed it with vanilla and honey and served it with crunchy toasted almonds and sweet berries. Everyone loves it!

2 tablespoons unsalted butter

3 tablespoons blanched sliced almonds

⅛ teaspoon fleur de sel

⅓ cup pure maple syrup

2 cups Homemade Ricotta (recipe follows)

2 tablespoons honey

1 teaspoon pure vanilla extract

1 pint mixed berries, such as raspberries, blueberries, and strawberries

Toasted brioche or challah, for serving

Melt the butter in a small sauté pan over medium heat. Stir in the almonds and sauté, tossing frequently, for 2 to 3 minutes, until the almonds are golden brown. Sprinkle with the fleur de sel, add the maple syrup, and keep warm.

Meanwhile, combine the ricotta, honey, and vanilla and divide it among breakfast plates. Surround the ricotta with the berries and spoon the almond and maple syrup mixture over the ricotta. Place a slice of toasted brioche on each plate and serve warm.

MAKE IT AHEAD: Prepare the ricotta and refrigerate for up to 5 days. Make the almond topping, toast the bread, and assemble before serving.

Homemade Ricotta MAKES 2 CUPS

4 cups (1 quart) whole milk
2 cups (1 pint) heavy cream
1 teaspoon kosher salt
3 tablespoons good white wine vinegar

Set a medium-mesh sieve over a deep bowl. Line the sieve with two double layers of cheesecloth and dampen the cheesecloth.

Pour the milk and cream into a large stainless-steel or enameled pot such as a Le Creuset and stir in the salt. Bring to a full rolling boil over medium heat, stirring occasionally (a full rolling boil means that you can't stir the mixture down with a spoon). Turn off the heat and pour in the vinegar. Allow the mixture to stand for one minute, until it curdles.

Pour the mixture into the cheesecloth-lined sieve and allow it to drain into the bowl, discarding the liquid as it collects in the bowl. Allow the mixture to drain at room temperature for 20 to 25 minutes. The longer you allow it to drain, the thicker it will be. Transfer the ricotta to another bowl, discarding the cheesecloth and any liquid. Use immediately or cover with plastic wrap and refrigerate.

Maple Vanilla Cream of Wheat serves 8 to 10

Lidey Heuck works with me and she was reminiscing about the delicious vanilla cream of wheat they would serve on Wednesday mornings at Bowdoin College, where she went to school. This is my version and trust me, it's worth getting out of bed for on a cold winter morning!

I love grade A dark amber pure maple syrup—it has a complex sweet and smoky flavor.

4 cups (1 quart) whole milk

2 cups (1 pint) half-and-half

2 cups water

3 tablespoons light brown sugar

2 tablespoons pure maple syrup (see note)

2 teaspoons kosher salt

1½ cups cream of wheat cereal (not instant)

1 teaspoon pure vanilla extract

Butter, maple syrup, and milk, for serving

Combine the milk, half-and-half, water, brown sugar, maple syrup, and salt in a very large saucepan and bring to a boil. Lower the heat and very slowly sprinkle on the cream of wheat, whisking constantly, until it's all incorporated. Simmer for 3 minutes, stirring constantly with a wooden spoon, until it's thickened. Stir in the vanilla and serve hot in bowls with a pat of butter, a drizzle of maple syrup, and cold milk.

MAKE IT AHEAD: Combine the ingredients from the milk to the salt in a pot and refrigerate. When ready to serve, bring to a boil, whisk in the cereal, and finish the recipe.

Overnight Belgian Waffles

MAKES 10 TO 12 LARGE WAFFLES

For years, I've tried unsuccessfully to make those big thick yeasty waffles that I've had in Belgium. Finally, I realized that the batter wasn't the problem, I needed a special waffle iron! The batter for these delicious waffles is made the night before and left on the counter for the flavors to develop. I serve them with bananas, toasted coconut, and maple syrup but you can top them with whatever you love!

If you don't have a Belgian waffle iron, you can use a standard waffle iron.

½ cup warm water (110 to 115 degrees)
1 package (¼ ounce) active dry yeast, at room temperature
2 teaspoons sugar
2 cups lukewarm whole milk (90 to 100 degrees)
¼ pound (1 stick) unsalted butter, melted, plus extra for the waffle iron
2 tablespoons honey
1 teaspoon pure vanilla extract
1¼ teaspoons kosher salt
2 cups all-purpose flour
2 extra-large eggs
¼ teaspoon baking soda
Sliced bananas, toasted coconut, warm maple syrup, and crème fraîche, for serving

I use an instant-read thermometer to test the hot water and milk.

The night before, combine the water, yeast, and sugar in a very large bowl (the batter will expand enormously). Allow it to stand for about 5 minutes, until the yeast dissolves and the mixture has started to foam, which tells you the yeast is active. Stir in the milk, butter, honey, vanilla, and salt. Add the flour and whisk until the batter is smooth. Cover the bowl with plastic wrap and allow it to sit overnight at a cool room temperature.

The next morning, heat a Belgian waffle iron according to the manufacturer's instructions and brush the top and bottom with melted butter. Beat the eggs together with the baking soda and whisk them into the batter until combined. Pour just enough of the batter onto the hot waffle iron to cover the grids (⅓ to ½ cup each, depending on your waffle maker), close, and cook for 5 to 6 minutes on medium heat, until the waffles are golden brown.

MAKE IT AHEAD: The waffles can be cooked up to 1 hour ahead and allowed to sit on sheet pans at room temperature. Reheat for 10 minutes in a 350-degree oven, turning once, before serving.

Cut them apart with a small knife, if necessary, and remove them with a fork. Repeat the process until all the batter has been used. Serve the waffles hot with sliced bananas, toasted coconut, maple syrup, and crème fraîche and let everyone help themselves.

Strawberry Rhubarb Compote
with Greek Yogurt SERVES 4

*This is like fruit and yogurt for breakfast, only better. The strawberry
rhubarb preserves are really easy to make and you serve them on a big
dollop of thick Greek yogurt.*

1 pound fresh strawberries
2 cups fresh rhubarb, ¾-inch-diced (¾ pound)
1½ cups sugar
1 tablespoon freshly squeezed lemon juice
Pinch of kosher salt
1 teaspoon grated orange zest
17 ounces Greek yogurt, for serving
Good granola, such as Bola, for serving

*Be sure to use a thermometer so
the preserves reach 220 degrees.*

Hull the strawberries and cut them in half or, if large, in quarters. Place the strawberries and rhubarb in a small (9-inch)
heavy-bottomed pot and heat over medium-high heat. Cook for
5 minutes, stirring occasionally, until the juices release from the
fruit and start to boil. (Winter fruit doesn't release as much juice
as it does in the summer so you may need to add ¼ cup of water.)
The fruit should still retain most of its shape. Off the heat, stir
in the sugar, lemon juice, and salt and stir to combine. Cover
the pot tightly and allow the preserves to sit overnight at room
temperature.

   The next day, bring the preserves to a boil, then lower the heat
and simmer for 10 to 15 minutes, until the mixture thickens (it
will be about 220 degrees on a candy thermometer). Stir in the
orange zest and serve warm or cold spooned over Greek yogurt
and sprinkled with granola.

MAKE IT AHEAD: Prepare the
preserves and refrigerate for
up to a week. Assemble
before serving.

Mini Italian Frittatas MAKES 12

Frittatas are a great way to serve eggs to a crowd. These frittatas are baked individually in muffin pans so everyone gets their own. They have lots of flavor from leeks, prosciutto, spinach, and Fontina Val d'Aosta.

2 tablespoons good olive oil, plus extra for greasing the pans

1½ cups chopped leeks, white and light green parts, washed and spun dry

4 ounces sliced Italian prosciutto, coarsely chopped (see note)

8 ounces fresh baby spinach

2½ tablespoons julienned fresh basil leaves

1 tablespoon freshly squeezed lemon juice

1½ cups (4 ounces) grated Italian Fontina cheese (6 ounces with rind)

8 extra-large eggs

1½ cups half-and-half

Kosher salt and freshly ground black pepper

4 tablespoons freshly grated Parmesan cheese

If the prosciutto sticks to the wrapping paper, heat it for 5 seconds in a microwave.

Preheat the oven to 375 degrees. Brush a standard 12-cup muffin tin with olive oil, including the top of the pan.

Heat the olive oil over medium heat in a large (12-inch) sauté pan. Add the leeks and sauté for 3 minutes, until tender. Add the prosciutto and sauté for 2 to 3 minutes, breaking it up with a fork. Add the spinach, tossing with tongs, then cover the pan and cook for 3 minutes, tossing once while it cooks, until the spinach is all wilted. Off the heat, stir in the basil and lemon juice and set aside for 5 minutes. Divide the mixture with tongs among the 12 muffin cups, leaving any liquid behind. Sprinkle the Fontina evenly on top.

In a 4-cup liquid measuring cup, beat the eggs, half-and-half, ½ teaspoon salt, and ¼ teaspoon pepper together with a fork. Pour the egg mixture evenly over the filling in each cup, filling the muffin cups to the top. Sprinkle each frittata with the Parmesan cheese.

MAKE IT AHEAD: Bake the frittatas, then cool, cover, and refrigerate for up to a day. Reheat for 15 minutes in a 350-degree oven.

Bake the frittatas for 20 to 25 minutes, until puffed and lightly browned on top. If you insert a toothpick in the middle, they should feel firm. Cool for 5 minutes, remove with a small sharp knife onto a serving plate, and serve hot or warm.

Make-Ahead Salt & Pepper Biscuits

MAKES 8 TO 10 BISCUITS

Lee Bailey was a great cookbook author and host. He often served baking powder biscuits with dinner but I also love them for breakfast with scrambled eggs. This is a twist on Lee's original recipe; I've added flaked sea salt and coarsely ground black pepper.

2 cups all-purpose flour
1 tablespoon baking powder
1 teaspoon kosher salt
6 tablespoons (¾ stick) cold unsalted butter, diced
⅔ cup cold half-and-half
1 extra-large egg beaten with 1 tablespoon half-and-half,
   for egg wash
Flaked sea salt, such as Maldon
Coarsely ground black pepper

Preheat the oven to 450 degrees. Line a sheet pan with parchment paper.

Place the flour, baking powder, and salt in the bowl of a food processor fitted with the steel blade and pulse to combine. Add the butter, breaking up the pieces as you put them in. Pulse the mixer about 10 times, until the butter is the size of large peas. With the mixer running, pour the half-and-half down the feed tube and pulse just until the mixture starts to come together.

Dump the dough out onto a floured board and quickly knead it into a ball. Roll the dough out ½ inch thick with a floured rolling pin. (You should see bits of butter in the dough.) Cut out biscuits with a 2½-inch plain round biscuit cutter and place them on the sheet pan. Brush the tops of the biscuits with the egg wash and sprinkle with the sea salt and pepper. Bake for 10 to 15 minutes, until browned and the biscuits are baked through. Allow to cool for 5 minutes and serve warm or at room temperature.

MAKE IT AHEAD: Roll the dough out, cut the biscuits, and refrigerate overnight. Brush with egg wash, sprinkle with salt and pepper, and bake before serving.

Blueberry Bran Muffins MAKES 12 MUFFINS

At Barefoot Contessa, we used to make literally thousands of muffins every morning. Most bran muffins taste like a cardboard box but these are moist, delicious, and filled with yogurt and blueberry goodness.

½ cup vegetable oil, plus extra for greasing the pan

1 cup all-purpose flour

1 teaspoon kosher salt

½ teaspoon baking powder

½ teaspoon baking soda

½ teaspoon ground cinnamon

7 ounces Greek yogurt

½ cup sugar

½ cup honey

2 extra-large eggs, lightly beaten

1 teaspoon pure vanilla extract

2½ cups wheat bran (see note)

1½ cups fresh blueberries (8 ounces)

Wheat bran is sometimes called miller's bran.

Preheat the oven to 350 degrees. Brush the top of a muffin pan with vegetable oil and line it with 12 paper liners.

Stir together the flour, salt, baking powder, baking soda, and cinnamon in a medium bowl. In a large bowl, whisk together the yogurt, sugar, ½ cup vegetable oil, honey, eggs, and vanilla until combined. Add the dry ingredients, stirring just until combined. Gently stir in the wheat bran and blueberries until combined.

Scoop the batter into the muffin cups with a rounded 2¼-inch ice cream scoop. Bake for 25 to 30 minutes, until the tops are golden brown and a cake tester comes out clean. Allow to cool for 5 minutes and serve warm or at room temperature.

MAKE IT AHEAD: Prepare the muffin batter and refrigerate overnight. In the morning scoop into muffin pans and bake.

Raspberry Baked French Toast serves 8 to 10

When I have company for the weekend, it's nice to serve something special for Sunday breakfast. This is basically a bread pudding made with all the ingredients I'd use to make French toast, but I can assemble it the night before and bake it in the morning. Vanilla, orange zest, and fresh raspberries give this great flavor!

If the bread isn't day-old, slice it 1 inch thick, place on a sheet pan, bake at 350 degrees for 5 minutes, turn, and bake for 5 more minutes.

1 tablespoon unsalted butter, at room temperature
10 extra-large eggs
2¾ cups half-and-half
⅓ cup plus 2 tablespoons granulated sugar
⅓ cup light brown sugar, lightly packed
1 tablespoon pure vanilla extract
1 teaspoon grated orange zest, plus extra for serving
½ teaspoon kosher salt
10 cups (1-inch-diced) day-old challah bread (see note)
12 ounces fresh raspberries
Confectioners' sugar, for serving
Pure maple syrup, for serving

Grease a 9 × 13 × 2-inch oval baking dish with the butter and set aside. In a large bowl, whisk together the eggs, half-and-half, ⅓ cup of granulated sugar, the brown sugar, vanilla, orange zest, and salt.

Spread half of the diced bread in the prepared baking dish. Sprinkle on the raspberries in one layer. Top with the rest of the bread and pour on the egg mixture, pressing down lightly to moisten the bread. Sprinkle with the remaining 2 tablespoons of sugar, cover with plastic wrap, and refrigerate for 1 hour.

Preheat the oven to 350 degrees. Place the baking dish on a sheet pan and bake it for 60 to 70 minutes, until the custard is set and the top is puffed and browned. Check after 45 minutes; if the top is getting too browned, cover it lightly with aluminum foil. Cool for 10 minutes, sprinkle with confectioners' sugar, dust with extra orange zest, and serve warm with maple syrup.

MAKE IT AHEAD: Assemble the dish and refrigerate overnight. Bake before serving.

Chocolate Banana Crumb Cake serves 9

When we tested this recipe, we all couldn't stop eating it! The combination of banana, chocolate, and streusel is irresistible.

¼ pound (1 stick) unsalted butter, at room temperature

¾ cup granulated sugar

1 extra-large egg, at room temperature

1 teaspoon pure vanilla extract

1½ cups mashed banana (3 to 4 very ripe bananas) (see note)

¼ cup sour cream

1½ cups all-purpose flour

1 teaspoon baking powder

¾ teaspoon baking soda

½ teaspoon kosher salt

FOR THE STREUSEL TOPPING

¾ cup light brown sugar, lightly packed

½ cup all-purpose flour

1½ teaspoons ground cinnamon

¼ teaspoon kosher salt

4 tablespoons (½ stick) unsalted butter, at room temperature

6 ounces bittersweet chocolate, chopped

3 tablespoons sliced blanched almonds

I mash bananas on a cutting board with a dinner fork.

Preheat the oven to 350 degrees. Grease and flour an 8 × 8 × 2-inch square baking pan.

In the bowl of an electric mixer fitted with the paddle attachment, cream the butter and sugar together on high speed for 3 minutes, until light and fluffy. Scrape down the bowl with a rubber spatula. With the mixer on low, beat in the egg, vanilla, banana, and sour cream and mix until combined. Don't worry—it may look curdled. In another bowl, sift together the flour, baking powder, baking soda, and salt. With the mixer on low, slowly add the dry ingredients to the wet ones. Scrape into the prepared pan and smooth the top.

For the streusel, combine the brown sugar, flour, cinnamon, salt, and butter in a medium bowl and pinch the ingredients together with your fingers until the mixture makes crumbles.

MAKE IT AHEAD: Bake the cake, wrap well, and allow it to sit at room temperature overnight.

Add the chocolate and combine. Distribute the streusel evenly over the batter, sprinkle the almonds on top, and bake for 40 to 45 minutes, until a cake tester inserted in the center comes out clean. Cool in the pan and serve warm or at room temperature.

make-ahead menus

summer breakfast
Fresh Orange Juice
Overnight Belgian Waffles
Fresh Fruit Plate
Sour Cream Coffee Cake (*Parties*)

birthday brunch
Mini Italian Frittatas
Bagels & Smoked Salmon
Cream Cheese
Lemon Ginger Molasses Cake

labor day lunch
Herbal Iced Tea (*Family Style*)
Zucchini & Goat Cheese Tart
Summer Paella Salad
Vanilla Semifreddo with Raspberry Sauce

ladies who lunch
Bellinis (*At Home*)
Roasted Kale
Crunchy Iceberg Salad with Creamy Blue Cheese
Salty Oatmeal Chocolate Chunk Cookies
Iced Coffee

fireside dinner
Slow-Roasted Spiced Pork
Maple Baked Beans (*At Home*)
Winter Slaw
Sour Cream Corn Bread
Coffee Granita

holiday dinner
Warm Fig & Arugula Salad
Herbed Pork Tenderloins with Apple Chutney
Roasted Brussels Sprouts (*BC Cookbook*)
Make-Ahead Goat Cheese Mashed Potatoes
Fresh Apple Spice Cake

july 4th celebration
Summer Rosé Sangria
Summer Filet of Beef with Béarnaise Mayonnaise
Sautéed Sugar Snap Peas
Summer Vegetable Couscous
Tri-Berry Crumbles

anniversary dinner
Tomatoes & Burrata
Moroccan Lamb Tagine
Steamed Couscous
Chocolate Cake with Mocha Frosting

For more recipes you can make ahead, go to BarefootContessa.com.

index

index

Note: Page references in *italics* indicate recipe photographs.

recipe index